Cats Are Weird

Unraveling the Secrets of Cat Behavior

L.R.Susko

Table of Contents

Introduction

Welcome to a journey through the enigmatic world of felines in "Cats are Weird: Unraveling the Secrets of Cat Behavior" by L.R. Susko. This book delves into the peculiarities and charms that make cats one of the most beloved and mystifying pets around the globe. With insightful observations and scientific explanations, L.R. Susko sheds light on the commonly baffling actions and habits of these graceful creatures. Whether you're a seasoned cat owner or simply a curious observer, this book promises to enhance your understanding and appreciation of your feline companions. Prepare to be both entertained and educated as we explore the fascinating behaviors of cats.

For Luka and Mutchka on the other side of
the rainbow bridge.

Decoding Feline Quirks

E ver caught yourself questioning the mysterious ways of your feline overlord? Perhaps you've noticed your cat assuming that peculiar "loaf" position on your favorite armchair, front paws tucked neatly beneath its body, resembling the world's cutest loaf of bread. While you're left wondering if they're just trying to make themselves look more scrumptious, there's actually a lot more to this quirky behavior, and it's rather fascinating.

Cats aren't just cuddling up for comfort when they tuck their paws; it's an intricate blend of instincts and practicalities. So, why hide the murder mittens? Picture this: in the wild, tucking those delicate paws under their fluffy bodies could be a matter of survival. Cats naturally protect their paw pads from the biting cold or potential threats by keeping them safely hidden. Much like how we'd curl up under a thick blanket on a chilly night, cats do the same to retain warmth and guard their most sensitive parts. It's evolution at its coziest!

In this chapter, we'll dive deep into the delightful world of feline loafing. From understanding the reasons behind this bread-like behavior to creating an inviting environment that encourages your cat to feel safe and secure, you're about to become a bona fide expert in decoding one of your pet's most endearing quirks. Get ready to uncover the science behind why your cat turns into a warm, fluffy loaf and how you can enhance their comfort and well-being, all while strengthening the bond you share with your whiskered bub.

The Science Behind the Loaf

Understanding why cats tuck in their paws while resting can be a furry little mystery. Neatly perched on the couch, paws tucked under their body, this adorable pose is known as "loafing," and it tells us a lot about our pet's comfort and security.

You see, cats are natural-born protectors of their paw pads. Much like how we humans tuck our hands into our pockets or even under our armpits for warmth, cats instinctively pull their paws beneath them to shield these areas. This tucking behavior can be traced back to wild instincts where keeping those crucial parts safe could mean the difference between life and death during harsh weather or threats from insect bites or a bigger animal trampling.

But it's not just about protection; it's also a matter of thermoregulation. Cats often tuck their paws in to keep warm, minimizing heat loss through their extremities. Their paws are particularly vulnerable to losing heat, and by curling up into a compact shape, they manage to conserve body heat efficiently. Think of it as nature's built-in eco-friendly heating system. Some humans instinctively sniff their fingers after an armpit tuck. The goal not being thermoregulation, more like sweat detection, but humans are strange beings too. At least we have great company! Weird is, as weird does.

When you observe a cat in the loaf position, it's a good sign they feel quite relaxed and secure. Cats won't assume this pose if they're feeling threatened or anxious. So, seeing your kitty loitering around in loaf mode is akin to receiving positive feedback on their level of contentment. It's their way of saying, "I'm comfortable here, I trust my environment."

Now, let's pivot to how you can create an inviting space that encourages this loafing behavior, enhancing your cat's overall well-being. Here's what you can do:

- First, provide cozy, secure resting spots. A soft blanket or a dedicated cat bed in a quiet corner can be incredibly appealing. Just like your keyboard or an empty box, there are some things those loafers can't resist.

- Second, ensure these spots are warm but not overly so. Cats love warmth, but you don't want them overheating.

- Third, consider placing these cozy nooks at varying heights. Some cats enjoy high perches where they can loaf and survey their kingdom from above.

Encouraging your cat to exhibit their natural loafing behavior isn't just about creating physical comfort; it's also about nurturing their mental well-being. By providing these snug resting areas, you're fostering a sense of security and promoting relaxation, much like setting up your perfect chill-out zone after a long day.

On another whisker-related note, it's interesting to compare this behavior with how cats handle other quirky habits. Ever noticed how they seem to curl up into tighter balls when they're sleeping on colder surfaces? This isn't far removed from "loafing." It all circles back to conserving warmth and feeling protected. In fact, research shows that animals instinctively adopt positions that help them maintain optimal body temperatures (ASPCA Professional, 2017).

These loafing cues are subtle indicators of your cat's state of mind. When they're sprawled out with their belly exposed, they're exhibiting a level of trust and comfort that's heartwarming to witness. Contrast this with the loaf position, which, while still a sign of contentment, is slightly more reserved. Understanding these nuances helps build a stronger bond with your feline companion.

Interestingly, the loaf position can also signal that your cat might be conserving energy for activities later. It's their version of going into low-power mode, storing up vitality for a burst of playfulness. This behavior stems from their predatory ancestors who needed to be ready to spring into action at a moment's notice. The domestic cat may have left the wild behind, but those instincts remain hardwired into their DNA.

Let's add a sprinkle of whimsy here. Imagine your cat channeling their inner ninja, poised in loaf stance—calm, collected, and ready to pounce on that unsuspecting toy mouse or an agile feather wand dangling nearby. Their preparation is methodical; loaf now, play later. It's a brilliant balance between serenity and spontaneity, encapsulating the very essence of being a cat.

Providing opportunities for your cat to engage in dynamic activities following their loaf-time is also beneficial. Environmental enrichment, such as interactive toys or puzzle feeders, can stimulate their minds and bodies. Cats might not need to hunt for survival anymore, but their drive to stalk, chase, and capture remains robust. Supporting these behaviors through playtime can mimic the rewards they'd naturally seek in the great outdoors.

As you observe these loafing sessions, you become attuned to your cat's rhythms and routines. Knowing when your cat tends to loaf can offer deeper insights into their daily patterns and preferences. Are they morning loafers, taking a gentle pause before the day's feline antics begin? Or perhaps they prefer evening loafs, winding down after a spirited afternoon. Each cat's loafing schedule is unique, painting a broader picture of their individual personality.

Being mindful of these details can enhance the relationship between you and your pet. It allows you to cater to their intrinsic needs, making their domestic environment as fulfilling as possible. After all, a happy cat often means a happier home.

To round things off, let's celebrate the simple joy of loafing. While it might appear mundane, it offers a window into the wonderful world of feline psychology—how they find comfort, manage their energy, and express contentment. Encouraging this behavior through cozy resting spots is a small but impactful way to show you care.

So, next time you see your kitty loafing away, take a moment to appreciate the contentment radiating from that furry bundle of joy. Perhaps even join them in a quiet moment of relaxation. After all, there's something quite special about sharing these small, serene snippets of life with a beloved pet.

And remember, whether your cat is performing acrobatics mid-air or channeling tranquility in a loaf pose, every behavior is a piece of the larger puzzle that makes them uniquely endearing.

Unraveling the Mystery of Cat Pouncing Behavior

Cats, with their enigmatic and whimsical behaviors, have often left us puzzled. Among the most captivating of these antics is their tendency to pounce on unseen objects. But what drives them to do so? Unraveling this mystery lies in understanding their predatory instincts and the myriad ways they engage with an environment that often seems invisible to us.

Cats' predatory instincts are deeply rooted in their DNA. Historically, cats were domesticated to control rodent populations, a role that required them to hone their hunting skills. Despite being well-fed pets today, this primal drive persists (FOUR PAWS International - Animal Welfare Organisation, n.d.). When your cat lunges at thin air or stalks imaginary prey, it's not losing its mind; rather, it's finely tuning agility and coordination. This practice, vital in the wild for survival, manifests in playful pouncing within our homes. Your living room becomes their savannah, every shadow, a potential hunt.

This behavior serves another critical purpose: mental stimulation. Pouncing on phantom prey keeps cats entertained and engaged. It's a form of play that's spontaneous, voluntary, and downright pleasurable for them (Kmecová et al., 2021). Consider it a feline version of solving puzzles or engaging in sports. They're not just making random leaps; they're maintaining cognitive sharpness and ensuring their minds remain as nimble as their bodies.

However, the modern indoor lifestyle can sometimes stifle these natural inclinations, leading to boredom and anxiety in our furry friends. Here's where you come into play. Providing interactive toys or engaging with feather wands can significantly satisfy a cat's innate need to stalk and pounce. A feather wand can mimic fluttering like a bird against the backdrop of your couch, drawing out those precise, instinctual movements from your cat.

Here's what you can do to keep your cat happy and mentally stimulated:

- Introduce interactive toys that mimic real prey, such as mice replicas or feather wands.
- Vary the types of toys to keep things interesting. Some days it could be laser pointers, other days crinkly balls.
- Engage in daily play sessions, ensuring you switch up the game to simulate a more natural hunting scenario.
- Rotate toys regularly to maintain novelty and avoid predictability.
- Ensure the play area is safe and free of small objects that could pose a choking hazard.

Understanding and appreciating a cat's pouncing behavior elevates the bond between owner and pet. Imagine seeing your feline friend not just as a cute companion but as a miniature predator, fulfilling its wild side in the safety of your home. By recognizing this intrinsic need, you're not just preventing behavioral issues; you're also enriching your pet's life. Engaging them in play strengthens your connection, making each day a new chapter in your mutual story.

So, the next time your cat suddenly freezes, eyes dilated, before launching an airborne attack on invisible prey, take a moment to appreciate this animistic echo from their past. Their seemingly whimsical behavior is a testament to the remarkable blend of instinct, intelligence, and playfulness that makes cats such brilliant companions.

While our feline friends indulge in their imagined safaris, we too are reminded of the simplicity and joy that comes from play. Cats teach us that even in a room full of nothing, there's always something worth chasing.

Why Cats Love Small Spaces

Why are cats irresistibly drawn to boxes like a magnet to metal? The answer is deeply rooted in their evolutionary history, going back thousands of years. This somewhat weird behavior may seem perplexing at first glance, but when we dig deeper and look at the evidence, it makes perfect sense. Imagine for a moment an ancient wildcat prowling the Fertile Crescent, seeking both prey and refuge in tight spots. Enclosed spaces offered security from larger predators and a vantage point to ambush unsuspecting rodents.

Fast forward to our modern-day furry friends, the instinct still runs strong. Our domestic cats, or felis catus as we'd call them in scientific parlance, feel secure in small, confined spaces. When they curl up inside a cardboard box, they're harking back to their wild ancestors' survival tactics. These behaviors have barely changed since those early days (Alley Cat Allies, n.d.). It's like watching an ancient play unfold on your living room floor.

The snug fit of a box gives cats a sense of boundaries and refuge, akin to having their very own mini fortress. This is not just a cozy nook; it's a structured environment that reduces stress and promotes relaxation. Think about how you feel in a warm, cozy blanket fort—you're cut off from the world's chaos, which makes everything better. That's precisely what a box does for a cat. Stress reduction in cats is crucial for their overall health. Studies show that providing multiple hiding spots —such as boxes—can significantly lower their anxiety levels and enhance their well-being (Bánszegi et al., 2020). Cat philosophy simplified: if it fits, I sits.

Allowing access to boxes or enclosed areas can serve as a form of environmental enrichment, promoting mental well-being in cats. Here's what you can do to create this enriching environment:

- Place different sizes of boxes around your home to provide your cat with options.

- Introduce these boxes gradually to let your cat get comfortable exploring each one.

- Add soft blankets or familiar toys inside the boxes to make them even more appealing.

- Rotate the boxes every few weeks to keep the experience novel and engaging for your feline friend.

Just imagine a little treasure hunt designed specifically for your cat! This simple act can transform their environment into a stimulating playground where they can explore and feel safe simultaneously. Adding to the adventure by switching things up keeps your kitty mentally active and happy.

Providing multiple hiding spots throughout the home can cater to a cat's natural inclination to seek out secluded spaces. It's not just about placing a box here or there; it's about understanding their need to hide and how you can fulfill it. Try considering these approaches:

- Place a couple of boxes in low-traffic areas of your house where your cat can retreat and relax without being disturbed.
- Utilize furniture, like cat trees with built-in cubbyholes, which offer vertical spaces for hiding.
- Hidey-holes near windows can serve as dual-purpose spots for both relaxation and bird-watching.

Giving your cat various hiding options ensures they always have a go-to spot regardless of their mood or the time of day. You've probably noticed that your cat's fascination with boxes goes beyond just sitting in them—they scratch, pounce, and play around them. This behavior adds another layer of understanding. Boxes aren't just safe havens; they are also prime real estate for play. Engaging in such activities inside and around boxes emulates their natural hunting instincts, allowing them to indulge in playful behaviors that keep them agile and sharp.

In essence, creating an environment that acknowledges and nurtures your cat's natural preferences isn't just good for their mental health —it has physical benefits as well. A mentally stimulated cat is less likely to exhibit behavioral issues like aggression or excessive meowing, contributing to a harmonious household.

Interestingly, there's empirical data supporting the value of confined spaces for cats in shelters. Behavioral tests on shelter cats have consistently shown that individual differences in behavior can be mitigated by offering environments rich in opportunities for hiding and playing (Bánszegi et al., 2020). This finding underscores the importance of these spaces for all cats, whether in shelter settings or homes.

Moreover, embracing this aspect of your cat's behavior can enrich your relationship with them. Witnessing the joy and comfort they derive from these simple pleasures brings us closer to understanding their world. This mutual sense of happiness is difficult to overestimate. Feeding their need for safety and security leads to a happier, healthier feline companion who is more content and easier to care for.

While we're at it, let's not forget the practicality of boxes from our perspective. They're affordable, easily replaceable, and recyclable. You don't need to break the bank to buy elaborate pet furniture when a sturdy cardboard box will do the trick just fine. Plus, it's a sustainable way to repurpose packaging materials, giving them a second life before recycling.

So, the next time you receive a delivery, don't rush to discard that box. Consider it a potential haven for your cat—a place where they can express their evolutionary instincts, find comfort, and enjoy a richer, more fulfilling life right at home.

To wrap it all up, providing a variety of boxes and cozy hiding places for your cat isn't just a whimsical indulgence; it's a thoughtful gesture grounded in our shared history with these creatures. By catering to their instinctual needs for security and comfort, you'll reduce their anxiety and enhance their overall happiness. And remember, each time your cat hops into a box, they're not just playing—it's an echo of a natural, age-old practice that's as vital today as it was millennia ago.

Unlocking the Secrets of Catnip and Feline Behavior

Catnip, also known as Nepeta cataria, is a member of the mint family and contains an enchanting compound called nepetalactone. This aromatic oil is what sends our feline friends into a tailspin of joy. Imagine your usually serene cat suddenly rolling, rubbing, or becoming exceptionally zany for a stretch of ten to fifteen minutes before mellowing out—catnip is often the culprit. Surprisingly, this euphoric response is a genetic trait, with about 50-70% of cats displaying sensitivity to its allure.

The reaction cats have to catnip can be quite the spectacle. Picture your furry friend catching a whiff and abruptly shifting from a nap on your favorite armchair to darting across the room, flipping over, and maybe even growling or meowing in heightened states of bliss. For others, it might take a quieter turn where they sniff, chew, and then relax into a zen-like state. Why does this happen? Well, when cats smell nepetalactone, it acts as a stimulant, targeting the "happy" receptors in their brains, much like how certain human recreational activities might offer a temporary escape from the mundane (The Humane Society of the United States, n.d.).

Interestingly, not all cats are susceptible to this reaction. The gene responsible typically kicks in between three to six months of age in kittens, just when they're getting ready to explore the world beyond the confines of their cozy beds. Until then, catnip remains just another herb to them.

Knowing that only a portion of our feline companions respond to catnip brings us to another intriguing aspect: heredity. Just like some humans will never be able to roll their tongues or curl their pinkies, around half of the cat population might never experience catnip-induced ecstasy. Researchers have found that the sensitivity to catnip is passed down through generations, making it a unique subject not just for pet owners but also for geneticists studying animal behavior (tamuvetmed, 2019).

However, it's essential to remember moderation. While catnip can provide an excellent source of mental stimulation and sensory enrichment, excessive exposure could lead to desensitization, rendering that once magical leaf nothing more than a wilted piece of foliage in your cat's eyes. Here's what you can do in order to keep catnip a delightful treat for your feline:

- Introduce catnip as an occasional treat rather than a regular part of their play routine.

- Observe your cat's reactions to gauge their enjoyment and any signs of overexposure.

- Store catnip in a cool, dry place to retain its potency for longer periods.

Keeping these guidelines in mind ensures that your cat continues to find joy and excitement in their little green treasure without reducing it to a mundane part of their day-to-day life.

The effects of catnip don't just stop at providing your cat with a short-lived high. New research by a team from Iwate University reveals that the molecules in catnip might serve a dual purpose. Iridoids, including nepetalactone, act as natural insect repellents, potentially protecting cats from pesky bites during their outdoor adventures (SITNFlash, 2024). Imagine that—the exuberant rolling around isn't just for show; it's a built-in bug repellent application process! Cats instinctively coat themselves with these compounds by licking, chewing, and rubbing against the plants, transferring the repellent onto their fur.

Another related plant, silver vine, also produces similar iridoids, causing the same frantic behavior in cats. Experiments conducted demonstrated that cats exposed to silver vine's nepetalactol showcased rolling and rubbing behavior akin to that seen with catnip. This behavior isn't merely about enjoying the scent but might involve activating the μ-opioid system in their brains, the same system that regulates pleasure and pain in humans (SITNFlash, 2024).

What does this mean for you and your feline buddy? Offering them occasional access to catnip or silver vine can enrich their lives, providing both mental stimulation and physical benefits. However, always be mindful, especially if it's their first encounter with the potent herb. Watch out for signs such as nausea or vomiting, which are clear indicators that your kitty has had too much of the good stuff. If these symptoms occur, you know it's time to dial back the catnip (tamuvetmed, 2019).

For those who want to go the extra mile, growing your own catnip could be a great project. Catnip thrives in most parts of North America and is relatively easy to care for. Having fresh catnip on hand means you can ensure its potency and quality, giving your companion the best of this herbal delight.

In summary, catnip isn't merely for laughs—though let's admit, watching your cat lose its mind over a bunch of leaves is incredibly entertaining. It's a powerful tool for enriching their environment and serving practical purposes like acting as a pest deterrent. Therefore, use it wisely, store it properly, and enjoy the sight of your cat engaging with one of nature's simplest yet most intriguing gifts.

Embracing the Whimsical World of Cats

So, to wrap up our deep dive into the whimsical behaviors of cats and their motivations, let's revisit the delightful mysteries we've been unraveling. We started by exploring why cats tuck their paws under themselves like little loaves of bread. They're not just being cute (though they excel at that); they're protecting those delicate paw pads and conserving body heat—a clever move inherited from their wild ancestors.

Speaking of wild instincts, we've also peeked into how cats' loafing positions reflect their comfort levels. When your cat curls up in loaf mode, it's a good sign they're feeling safe and content. Encouraging this behavior with cozy, warm resting spots can enhance their well-being, showing that sometimes, creating a perfect chill-out zone isn't just for us humans.

Now, let's link back to the wild side once more. The way cats handle thermal regulation is nothing short of fascinating. From curling into tight balls on cold surfaces to assuming the loaf pose, every movement is a fine-tuned dance to stay warm and protected. This blend of practicality and inherent cuteness can teach us so much about our furry companions' needs and preferences.

It's essential to address a concern pet owners might have: ensuring our indoor kitties get enough mental and physical stimulation. Just because they've traded the savannah for the sofa doesn't mean their predatory instincts have vanished. Providing interactive playtime and cozy spots caters to both their hunting drive and need for relaxation, ensuring a more enriched and fulfilling life for them.

On a broader scale, understanding and nurturing these natural behaviors has far-reaching consequences. A happy, mentally stimulated cat is less likely to develop behavioral issues, leading to a more harmonious home. Plus, observing and responding to their loafing habits strengthens your bond, making every snuggle session or playful pounce even more meaningful.

And so, as we marvel at our cats channeling their inner acrobats or serenity masters, remember each quirky habit is a window into their intricate world—a world where loafing around has never looked so charming. So next time you see your kitty in loaf stance, take a moment to appreciate the mix of instinct and trust wrapped in that fluffy bundle. Perhaps even join them in a quiet moment of zen, sharing the joy of simply loafing together. After all, in the whimsical realm of feline antics, there's always something new and delightful worth pondering.

Cat Communication Unleashed

E ver wonder if your cat is secretly plotting world domination or just trying to ask for more treats? While we can't completely unravel the enigma that is feline behavior, understanding cat communication can feel like gaining superpowers. Imagine transforming from an average cat owner to a whisker-whispering, tail-decoding extraordinaire! Grab your magnifying glass and deerstalker hat (metaphorically speaking), because you're about to embark on a journey into the mysterious world of cat communication.

Picture this: you walk into your living room, and your cat greets you with its tail held high, swishing back and forth like it's auditioning for a feline version of "Dancing with the Stars." Is it celebrating your grand entrance, or is it subtly reminding you that it runs the household? Is it actually trying to express it is happy to see you? YOU, yes you: the human that steals its excrement with a tiny shovel, then leaves. Then there are those times when the tail puffs up like a feather duster at the sight of the neighbor's dog, clearly signaling that something's amiss. It's fascinating how much information one fluffy appendage can convey! But hold onto your kibble, because it gets even more intricate. Tail movements, twitches, and contours form a silent language of their own, giving us glimpses into our cats' inner worlds.

In this chapter, we're diving deep into the realm of tail talk. From the triumphant tail held high to the enigmatic twitch, each movement tells a tale (pun very intended). We'll explore what a high-held tail signifies about feline confidence and happiness, decode the mixed messages behind those rapid twitches, and understand the theatrical puffed-out tail as a universal sign of fear or aggression. By the end, you'll not only be able to read your cat's emotional weather forecast—you'll also have the tools to respond appropriately, creating a harmonious living environment for both you and your whiskered companion. So, sit back, relax, and get ready to become a master in the art of cat communication!

The Language of Tail Movements

Delving into the intricate ways cats communicate can feel like deciphering an ancient, mystical code. Yet, it's a rewarding journey that brings us closer to our feline friends. Each flick, twitch, and puff of their tail offers a window into their inner world, providing us with invaluable insights into their emotions and needs.

First, let's talk about when a cat's tail is held high. This is more than just an adorable posture; it signifies confidence and happiness. Picture your cat strutting around with its tail held tall—in a way, it's their little victory lap around the house. It's almost as if they're saying, "I own this place, and I'm feeling good!" When you observe this behavior, it's a clear sign that your cat is comfortable and content in their environment. Think of it as your cat's version of a smile. According to research from PAWS Chicago, an erect tail serves as a greeting or a request for attention (PAWS Chicago, n.d.). By recognizing this signal, you can better understand your cat's emotional state and foster a stronger, happier bond.

Now, let's move on to tail twitching. Ah, the enigmatic tail twitch. At times, it can be a mere flick, almost unnoticeable; at other times, it's more pronounced—like a feather duster swishing back and forth. The Humane Society notes that tail thrashing often indicates agitation or anger (The Humane Society of the United States, n.d.). However, tail twitching can also signify excitement. Maybe your cat has spotted a toy, or perhaps they're gearing up for a playful pounce. It's essentially your cat broadcasting a mixed message: "I'm intrigued, but I could get annoyed very quickly." By paying attention to these subtle cues, you can anticipate your cat's next move and adjust your interactions accordingly—whether that means grabbing a toy for playtime or giving them some space.

Next is the tell-tale puffed-out tail. This is a universal sign for fear or aggression, much like a Halloween cat spookily arched and ready to defend itself: instant floof! When a cat's tail fluffs up, they're trying to make themselves look bigger, an instinctual defense mechanism against perceived threats. Imagine encountering a wild animal unexpectedly: you'd want to appear as formidable as possible. A puffed-out tail is your cat's way of doing just that. When you see this, approach with caution, or better yet, give them plenty of space to calm down. According to Cat Care Society, a bristled tail that is straight out or down is often a sign of aggression (Dokolasa, 2023).

Observing and understanding these tail movements don't just help in decoding what your cat is trying to convey; they also enhance your mutual communication. Reading these signals effectively can significantly improve your relationship with your cat. Here's a useful guideline to achieve this:

- Pay close attention to your cat's body language and context.
- Respond calmly to fearful or aggressive signals by giving your cat space.
- Use positive reinforcement like treats or gentle petting when your cat expresses confidence or happiness through their tail position.
- Avoid sudden movements or loud noises that might aggravate or trigger negative responses.

By incorporating these practices, not only will you become more attuned to your cat's moods, but you'll also create a more harmonious living environment.

Key takeaways? Reading a cat's tail language enhances communication and fosters a deeper understanding of their feelings. Trust me, getting clued into your cat's tail movements is like learning a new dialect—one that deepens the bond between you two.

Remember, every flick, wag, and puff of that tail is a part of a larger symphony of signals your cat uses to communicate. And by tuning into these subtle cues, you'll find your relationship with your feline companion growing richer, more nuanced, and infinitely more rewarding.

The Significance of Purring

Understanding the reasons behind a cat's purring and its significance in their communication can be an insightful journey for any cat owner. Purring is one of the most fascinating sounds that our feline friends make, and it isn't just limited to expressing contentment. Let's dig deeper into what those delightful vibrations truly mean.

Cats purr when content or seeking comfort, showing their trust and affection towards their human companions. Imagine sitting on your couch, reading a book, and your cat climbs onto your lap, curling up and starting to purr. That soft rumble signals a deep bond of trust, almost like they're whispering, "I feel safe with you." It's heartwarming, right? But here's where it gets interesting: cats don't only purr when they're happy.

Purring can also signal pain or distress, indicating the need for attention or medical intervention (Ahmed et al., 2020). This might come as a surprise, but it's true. If your usually playful kitty is hiding under the bed and purring continuously, it could be a sign that something's wrong. They may be telling you, "I need help." Here are some guidelines to help you respond appropriately:

- Observe if there are additional signs of discomfort such as limping, loss of appetite, or changes in behavior.

- Gently check for any visible injuries or abnormalities without causing further stress to your cat.

- If you notice persistent or unusual purring along with other symptoms, it's best to consult your veterinarian promptly.

Deciphering the context of purring aids in responding appropriately to the cat's emotional needs. It's like learning a new language, except this one involves fur and whiskers. When your cat purrs while rubbing against your leg, it's probably a request for more petting or perhaps a treat. On the flip side, if they're purring during a visit to the vet, it might be a self-soothing mechanism.

Recognizing different purring patterns helps in strengthening the human-cat relationship and promoting well-being. Think of it as tuning into different radio stations—each purr has its own frequency and meaning. A loud, consistent purr might indicate they're super relaxed. Conversely, a sporadic or urgent purr might require a bit more detective work on your part to understand what they need. Strengthening your bond with your cat isn't rocket science; it's about being attentive, patient, and empathetic.

Understanding the various meanings of purring enables effective communication and enhances the bond with the cat. Just as you would appreciate someone who understands your feelings and responds accordingly, your cat will thrive in an environment where their communicator's efforts are recognized and met with appropriate responses. Engaging with them not only fulfills their immediate needs but also nurtures a lasting and affectionate connection.

So, next time your cat curls up next to you and starts that rhythmic purring, take a moment to listen and observe. You'll find that each purr tells a story, and understanding those tales will bring you closer to your furry companion. It's these subtle nuances that make cat companionship so enriching. Whether it's a purred lullaby of contentment or a plea for help, being tuned into these vibrations will make you a better, more responsive pet parent.

In conclusion, delving into the intricate ways cats communicate through purring reveals a tapestry of emotions and needs they express daily. By paying close attention to the situation and responding appropriately, cat owners can ensure their pets' well-being while nurturing a deeper, more meaningful bond. Isn't it amazing how much can be said without words?

Decoding Vocalizations

Decoding the different vocalizations of cats and their significance in communication will aid in understanding those meows, trills, mips, and chuffs. When it comes to understanding our feline friends, one must pay close attention to their vocalizations. Meowing, for instance, can express various needs such as hunger, attention, or greetings. As a cat owner, it's crucial to become an attentive listener. Imagine your cat's meow morphing from a polite "Can I have some kibble?" to a more insistent "Human, feed me now! Meow!" Each type of meow carries with it a unique message that warrants deciphering.

So, how do you crack the code? By recognizing the pitch and tone of those meows. A high-pitched, urgent meow often signals hunger or discomfort, while softer, melodious meows usually indicate contentment and affection. You might think of it like tuning into different stations on a radio; each frequency tells you something different about your cat's emotional state. If the kitty is grumbling with a low, rumbly meow, it's time for some detective work to figure out what's bothering him.

Here is what you can do in order to achieve this goal:

- Pay close attention to the sound variations in your cat's meows.

- Note the context in which these vocalizations occur—during feeding times, when you come home, or right before using the litter box.

- Compare these instances and start identifying patterns in pitch and tone to better understand your cat's needs.

Different meow patterns also offer a wealth of information. For example, rapid, repetitive meows can convey excitement and playfulness. This could be your cat's way of saying, "Let's chase that laser pointer again!" or "More treats! More treats! More treats!" On the flip side, long, drawn-out meows might be distress calls—indicating anything from feeling trapped in a closet to experiencing pain. Recognizing these vocal cues can guide you in taking appropriate action to alleviate their concerns.

Here's how you can respond appropriately:

- Observe any accompanying body language. Is your cat's tail puffed up? Are the ears flattened?

- Check out the immediate environment. Is there something new or unsettling?

- Offer comfort when the meows suggest anxiety or fear. Sometimes, just being there can make all the difference.

- Offer your own vocalization as acknowledgement. Just no yelling as this will automatically put your cat on high-alert. You never know, you might just speak cat!

Exploring the nuances of meowing does more than improve your ability to meet your cat's basic needs. It also enhances communication and strengthens the bond between the two of you. After weeks of careful listening and observation, you practically become a feline translator. Your cat feels heard and understood, leading to fewer miscommunications and a stronger, happier relationship.

Interpreting a cat's vocalizations promotes effective communication and deepens the relationship with your feline companion. Once you've got the hang of discerning meows, you'll find yourselves engaging in delightful 'conversations.' And let's be honest, who wouldn't want to chat with the furry overlords of the household?

Consider the story of Whiskers and her human, Alex. Initially, Whiskers' meowing was just background noise. But upon closer inspection, Alex started to notice distinct differences in her vocal patterns. The excited trill when Alex returned home, the plaintive cry near dinner time, and even the soft purr-meow combo during cuddle sessions started making sense. Eventually, their bond became so strong that Whiskers anticipated Alex's routine just as much as Alex predicted Whiskers' moods.

Understanding these vocalizations isn't merely about reducing stress or preventing issues; it's about enhancing every interaction with your cat, turning mundane moments into meaningful exchanges. Next time your feline friend starts a meow-a-thon, listen closely. You might just discover a whole new layer of kitty charisma you never knew existed.

Understanding Body Language

When it comes to understanding cats and their complex world, one has to pay special attention to the non-verbal cues they use in communication. Let's dive into how these delightful creatures utilize body language to convey their feelings and intentions—not only to us but also to their feline friends. Cats do communicate with each other through non-verbal cues more than audible sounds. You might notice, meowing is more reserved for humans.

Body posture, ear movements, and eye contact offer deep insights into a cat's state of mind and intentions. For instance, when a cat's ears are facing forward and erect, it's usually a signal that the cat is curious or content. Imagine your cat sitting by the window, eyes wide open and ears perked up as if picking up every possible sound—it's likely just soaking in its surroundings with interest (Source 1: Cat Communication | International Cat Care). We've come to call the intricate ear movements of our cat as "radar ears" when highly alert and excited. The ears will move independently, creating some funny faces the cat is unaware we observe as amusing.

In contrast, sideways ears are like flashing red lights signaling potential trouble. If you see your cat's ears turned sideways, step back and evaluate what might be disturbing them. Maybe it's the loud vacuum cleaner, or perhaps an unfamiliar visitor. Either way, give them some space and time to calm down before attempting any interaction (Source 2: Decoding Cat Body Language | Cat Care Society).

Cats are masters at using slow blinks to communicate trust and affection, a gesture often missed by us humans. Think of it as the equivalent of a warm hug or a reassuring pat on the back. Here is what you can do to reciprocate this beautiful sign of love:

- Observe your cat's behavior; if it starts to blink slowly at you, try returning the favor by blinking slowly back.

- Ensure you're at a comfortable distance to avoid making your cat feel trapped.

- Maintain a relaxed posture yourself, which naturally puts your cat at ease.

- Avoid making sudden movements or loud noises during this exchange.

These slow blinks do wonders in building a sense of security and strengthening the bond between you and your feline friend. It is very easy to do. Make eye contact then close your eyes slowly and open them again in the same position. Don't be discouraged if your cat looks away. You just exchanged an "I love you." Sometimes that's all that needs to be said. It's one of those little things that goes a long way in fostering mutual trust, affection, and understanding. Cats do love to watch you in adoration, so don't feel uncomfortable about the staring. They will often look away if you make eye contact during their love-fest, after all prolonged mutual eye contact can be interpreted as a challenge or confrontation in the wild. So breaking eye contact is normal when they are busted. Imagine how sweet it is to be met with "I love you too" in the midst of their silent watching.

Now, shifting our gaze to tail positioning, whisker movements, and head gestures—the unsung heroes of inter-feline and human-feline communication. An upright tail often signals friendliness. It's like your cat saying, "Hey there! I'm in a good mood." or "Yo! Yo! Let's play!" On the other hand, a puffed-up tail is a classic sign of a cat feeling threatened. You've likely seen this during those unexpected encounters with the neighborhood dog. Your cat wants to appear larger and more intimidating than it actually is—a clever bit of biological drama (Source 1: Cat Communication | International Cat Care). Your cat might just run away and you'll find them puffed-up behind the washing machine acting like a frightened or angry ball of lint!

Whiskers, another vital communication tool, change positions based on the cat's emotions. When a cat's whiskers are relaxed and sticking out sideways, all is well in their world. Forward-pointing whiskers show curiosity, while whiskers flattened against the face indicate fear or anxiety. Once, my cat Luka had her whiskers pulled back while giving a sideways glance at an overly curious toddler—it was her polite yet firm way of asking for some personal space. she quickly exited shortly thereafter. She wanted to sniff the sticky hands, but knew they could be overly grabby and got out of there.

Understanding these silent cues enhances empathy, facilitates better communication, and strengthens the human-cat relationship. For example, how could I be unhappy Luka did not want to play with the toddler? She gave plenty of cues about her own feelings before she left and we understand the grabby hands lead to hair-pulling and other shenanigans. The more adept we become at recognizing what our cats are trying to tell us, the richer our interactions will become. By tuning into their subtle signs, not only do we become better guardians, but we also open doors to deeper connections filled with mutual respect and understanding.

Picture this: You come home after a tiring day, and your cat greets you with its tail held high, whiskers relaxed, and gives you those slow, trusting blinks. In that moment, you realize that both of you have developed a unique language, one that transcends verbal boundaries. It's a special relationship built on silent understanding, where both parties know they are cared for and appreciated. Yay! It is worthy a small celebration, a mental pat on the back, so to speak.

So next time you're around your furry friend, take a moment to observe. Their body language is a treasure trove of information just waiting to be unlocked. Whether it's the flick of a tail, the position of their ears, or the dilation of their pupils, each tells a story. And believe me, once you start "listening" to these stories, your bond with your cat will flourish in ways you never imagined.

Bridging the Communication Gap

In our delightful journey delving into the myriad ways cats communicate, we've danced through a symphony of tail flicks, mysterious purrs, intriguing meows, and expressive body language. It turns out, understanding your feline friend isn't so different from deciphering hieroglyphs—just with more fur, fewer pyramids, and no sand. Sand gets everywhere!

Remember when we first embarked on this adventure, discussing the significance of a cat's erect tail? It's their version of a victory lap, a confident "I own this place!" strut. Now, picture these moments as part of a broader tapestry, where twitching tails hint at excitement or agitation and puffed-out tails scream fear, all in an effort to convey their feelings. Who knew tails could be so chatty?

Then there's the enchanting realm of purring. Initially, we might think that soft rumble is simply a sign of kitty bliss as they curl up on our laps. But lo and behold, purring can also indicate discomfort or pain—their melodious SOS. It's kind of like discovering that your favorite song also doubles as an emergency siren. So next time your cat's purr seems off-key, keep an eye out for other signs of distress.

We've also decoded those endless meows— from melodic hunger serenades to insistent cries for attention. Understanding these vocal nuances can make you feel like you've earned a Ph.D. in

Feline Linguistics. Go, you! And beyond meowing, observing whiskers, ear positions, and even those slow blinks can offer profound insight into what's brewing in their furry little heads.

Our take-home message? Communication with our feline companions is a two-way street paved with curiosity, patience, and empathy. When you see that high-flying tail or hear a peculiar meow, you're not merely observing behaviors; you're engaging in a silent dialogue filled with trust and affection.

Concerns might arise about missing these subtle cues—what if you misread a purr or overlook a flicking tail? Fear not! Every interaction is a learning opportunity. The wider impact of mastering these communication skills goes beyond just preventing your favorite chair from becoming a scratch post. It enriches your relationship, turning you into a better, more attentive, responsive, and loving owner.

And here's the kicker: as you tune into these signals, you'll find yourself enchanted by the everyday moments—a slow blink here, an upright tail there. These moments form a tender narrative, deepening a bond built on mutual understanding.

So go ahead, embrace this weird and quirky, enlightening quest of decoding your cat's secret language. After all, isn't it magical how much love and connection can be found without uttering a single word?

Purr-sonality Traits Unmasked

I magine this: You walk into your living room, ready to unwind after a long day, only to find your cat perched atop the curtains like some sort of feline ninja. Meanwhile, your other cat is lounging on the couch, barely lifting an eyelid to acknowledge your arrival. It's easy to wonder if these two creatures share anything in common besides whiskers and a penchant for knocking things off tables. Welcome to the world of cats, where no two personalities are alike, and deciphering their quirks can feel like trying to solve a Rubik's Cube blindfolded.

The enigma of cat personalities often leaves owners scratching their heads—or scratching at all, if you've ever had a playful kitten confuse your toes for toys. Some cats demand attention like tiny divas, following you from room to room and vocalizing their every need with a series of insistent meows and chirps. Others seem to enjoy their solitude, peeking out from behind furniture as if they were plotting world domination or something more nefarious in your sleep. These personality differences shape how they interact not just with you, but with their entire surroundings. For instance, an introverted cat might find solace in quiet corners or high perches, while an extroverted furball might relish romping around the house and engaging with an array of interactive toys. Getting the balance right isn't just about keeping your cat happy; it's also about preserving your sanity—and maybe that antique vase or your glass of water.

In this chapter, we will pull back the curtain on the wide range of feline personalities and delve into how these traits impact their behavior and interactions with us human sidekicks. Expect to uncover tips on recognizing whether your cat is more of a social butterfly or a lone wolf, and how to tailor your approach to meet their unique needs. From creating cozy hideaways for the shy types to orchestrating epic play sessions for the energetic ones, you'll find strategies to keep your cat entertained, engaged, and ultimately happier. So strap in—because understanding your cat's personality is not just an art; it's also part science, part magic, and 100% worth it.

Understanding Cat Personalities and Their Impact on Behavior

When it comes to understanding the feline world, it's essential to acknowledge that our whiskered friends are just as nuanced as humans. Cats can fall anywhere on the introvert-extrovert spectrum, and this dramatically influences how they interact with their environment and their favorite "hoomans." Some cats might be the life of the party, craving constant attention and interaction, while others may prefer a quiet nook in the house, observing the hustle and bustle from afar with those enigmatic eyes.

The thing to remember is, there's no one-size-fits-all approach when it comes to cats' personalities. Whether your cat is a social butterfly or an independent thinker, recognizing these traits can help you tailor their environment and interactions to suit their needs.

If your cat is more of an introvert, consider creating cozy hideaways where they can retreat and feel secure. Boxes, high perches, or even a snug spot under the bed can become their sanctuary. For the extroverted cats who thrive on interaction, ensure they have plenty of toys, playtime, and opportunities to engage with you. Cats like James Bond—Blofeld's cat named Solomon for his secretive, but incredibly observant nature—demonstrate how an enriched environment tailored to their sociable traits can satisfy their need for stimulation (Serpell et al., n.d.).

Understanding your cat's personality doesn't just make life easier for them; it significantly enhances your bond and communication with them. Imagine trying to befriend someone without knowing what makes them tick—awkward, right? Similarly, knowing whether your cat is a talker or the silent, strong type can make all the difference in strengthening your relationship.

Here's what you can do in order to achieve this enhanced connection:

- Spend quality time observing your cat's behavior in various situations. Notice what makes them purr with joy or hiss with distaste.

- Interact with them using toys or activities that match their energy levels. A laser pointer might work wonders for an active cat, while a feather wand could captivate a more curious but less high-energy kitty.

- Pay attention to their body language and vocal cues. Understanding if a certain meow means "feed me" or "cuddle time" helps improve communication and respect between you both.

- Incorporate routine into their daily life. Predictability helps reduce stress, particularly for more anxious or introverted cats.

Speaking of different personalities requiring varying levels of attention and care, let's face it: some cats are high-maintenance divas while others are low-key lounge lizards. The diva requires hours of engagement, be it through play, petting, or verbal adoration. The lounge lizard is content sprawled out on the couch, soaking up rays with minimal interference. Both types are wonderful in their unique ways, but they do necessitate different approaches.

For example, a feline with a high score in Extraversion from the Feline Five personality traits (Chiera et al., 2017) will likely need more mental and physical stimulation than a cat scoring high in Neuroticism, who might benefit from extra hiding places and a quieter home environment.

Ensuring your cat's welfare needs based on their personality can also diminish behavioral issues. Siracusa often emphasizes that many so-called "behavior problems" stem from unmet environmental needs (Hakanen et al., 2021). If your cat tends to be destructive, it might not be disobedience but rather boredom or pent-up energy. By providing appropriate outlets, you're addressing the root cause rather than merely managing the symptoms.

By acknowledging and catering to your cat's distinct personality traits, you pave the way for a deeper, more fulfilling relationship. It becomes less about cohabiting with a mysterious creature and more about sharing a meaningful companionship where mutual understanding reigns supreme.

In sum, recognizing and respecting your cat's individuality transforms both your lives. They're not just pets—they're companions with their quirks, preferences, and moods. Whether they're peeking out from behind the curtains or demanding belly rubs in the middle of a conference call, these magical beings enrich our lives immeasurably, provided we take the time to understand them. So, here's to treating our furry friends with the same respect and consideration we extend to our human companions—after all, isn't that what love is all about?

Exploring Feline Attachment Styles

Let's delve into the world of feline attachment styles and how they shape their interactions with us. Every cat is its own charming enigma, but understanding their individual attachment styles can unlock a more harmonious and loving relationship between you and your whiskered friend.

Some cats are natural lone wolves, reveling in their independence, while others stick to you like velcro, craving constant companionship. Just as humans vary in their need for social interaction, so do our feline friends. Some might enjoy the freedom to roam and explore every nook and cranny of your home, while others may seek solace in your lap or curl up beside you at night. This spectrum of behavior is heavily influenced by their attachment style, which can range from aloof to affectionate.

Understanding your cat's unique attachment style doesn't require a degree in psychology, but it does call for some keen observation and empathy. If your cat's behavior sometimes mystifies or frustrates you, recognizing their attachment style can offer valuable insights and practical ways to address any issues. Here's what you can do:

- Pay close attention to patterns in their behavior. Does your cat shy away when you try to initiate petting, preferring to be self-sufficient? Or do they follow you around, meowing for attention?

- Notice how they react to changes in their environment or routine. Independent cats might take disruptions in stride, while more clingy cats could display signs of stress or anxiety.

- For problem behaviors like scratching furniture or not using the litter box, consider if these actions are a cry for more interaction or an expression of discontent. Tailoring your response with this understanding can foster a more secure bond.

Acknowledging these different attachment styles means creating a balance that caters to both your cat's needs and your own. Here's where finding the sweet spot between independence and affection comes into play:

- Set up an environment that provides opportunities for exploration and solo play, like interactive toys or high perches. These cater to their innate curiosity and provide mental stimulation for independent cats.

- Simultaneously, build moments of connection through regular interaction, such as play sessions with a feather toy or gentle petting. This will satisfy the emotional needs of those who are more affectionate.

Respecting your cat's natural inclination—whether they are the feline equivalent of a socialite or a hermit—is crucial. A thriving relationship blossoms from mutual respect and accommodation. You can enhance your living environment by taking small steps:

- Create safe spaces or hideaways where your cat can retreat to unwind and feel secure. This is especially comforting for independent cats who might need alone time.

- Engage in activities that align with their preferences. For instance, a cat that loves being petted might enjoy a thorough grooming session, while a more independent one might prefer engaging in a structured playtime.

- Allow your cat to dictate the pace and nature of their interaction with you. Being attuned to their signals, like whether their tail is swishing in irritation or gently flicking in contentment, can help you adjust your approach accordingly.

Research supports the idea that the way we interact with our pets can significantly impact their behavior and overall well-being. A study published by Hakanen et al. (2023) found that the personalities of both owners and pets contribute to the attachment styles in their relationships. Owners' levels of neuroticism, for example, can influence the type of attachment formed with their pets, underscoring the importance of understanding these dynamics.

Ultimately, it's about finding that equilibrium where both you and your feline companion can thrive. Recognizing and nurturing your cat's attachment style can turn everyday interactions into opportunities for building trust and love. So, whether your cat greets you at the door with enthusiastic meows or observes you from a distance with a regal gaze, embracing their unique personality is the key to a fulfilling companionship.

A crucial takeaway is that there's no one-size-fits-all approach when it comes to our furry friends. Each cat is a unique entity, shaped by its personality and experiences. By tuning into their individual needs and preferences, you not only address behavioral issues more effectively but also enhance the bond you share.

In essence, cats, with their myriad personalities and quirks, easily interpreted as weird, teach us to appreciate the beauty of individuality. By understanding and respecting their attachment styles, we open the door to a deeper, more empathetic relationship, filled with shared moments of joy and companionship. Who doesn't need more joy in their life?

So next time your cat bats at your fingers or curls up in your lap, remember: they're communicating in their own way. And by paying attention and responding appropriately, you're laying the groundwork for a friendship that enriches both your lives. Whether your kitty is a solitary hunter or a snuggle bug, celebrating their uniqueness is the secret sauce for a happy cohabitation. Enjoy the journey of discovery and revel in the special bond you create with your feline friend.

Personality Traits and Activity Levels in Cats

When it comes to cats, finding out what makes them tick can be as puzzling as deciphering hieroglyphics. Each feline furball has a unique personality that shapes its play preferences and activity levels. Understanding these quirks isn't just amusing—it's essential for their well-being. Let's dive into how recognizing and responding to your cat's character could turn you into the ultimate cat whisperer.

Some cats are bundles of energy. You know the type—dashing around the house at 3 AM like they've seen a ghost, batting at anything that moves (or doesn't), and generally acting like they've had one too many espressos. For these playful felines, interactive toys and engaging activities are life savers. It's not just about keeping them busy; it's about channeling that relentless energy into constructive fun. Besides, spending that energy makes it less likely you'll hear your cat have a 4am jam session singing the song of their people or get pounced upon while trying to sleep.

Here is what you can do in order to achieve the goal:

- Get toys that mimic prey behavior, like feather wands or laser pointers. Cats are natural hunters, so anything that moves unpredictably will catch their attention.

- Create DIY puzzles by hiding treats in boxes or using food-dispensing toys. This keeps their minds sharp and bodies active.

- Incorporate regular play sessions into your day. Playtime isn't just for kittens; adult cats need it too. Aim for multiple short bursts of play rather than long sessions. We joke it is time to put the toys away when it becomes an observational activity versus a recreational one, but this is a certain cue they are done, lost interest, or are worn out.

Cats, much like humans, can get bored. And a bored cat is a mischief-making machine. Understanding your cat's activity level is crucial to preventing boredom and the behavioral issues that come with it. Who hasn't walked into a room only to find their curtains shredded or their favorite potted plant mysteriously uprooted? These aren't just naughty behaviors—they're cries for stimulation.

To keep boredom at bay:

- Rotate toys regularly. Even the most exciting toy becomes mundane if it's always available.

- Offer a variety of textures and types of toys. Some cats prefer soft, plush toys while others love hard, plastic ones.

- Make use of vertical spaces like cat trees and shelves. Many cats love to climb and observe their kingdom from above.

On the flip side, some cats are more content being couch potatoes. They lounge in sunny spots, looking disdainfully at balls of yarn and feathery doodads. While it might be tempting to let them snooze away the day, lazy or less active cats benefit from gentle encouragement and stimulation.

Here is what you can do in order to achieve the goal:

- Engage them with slow-moving toys. Think of battery-operated mice that scuttle slowly across the floor or balls that roll gently. Balls of foil, the ring from around the top of plastic milk jugs, long twist ties or pipe cleaners bent into springs are examples of inexpensive, slow-moving toys which may get your cat's attention.

- Incorporate play into feeding time. Try scatter-feeding, where you toss kibble across the floor, making your cat work a bit for their meal.

- Use scent enrichment like catnip or silvervine to pique their interest. Sometimes a whiff of something intriguing is all it takes to get a paw moving. Try storing a few small toys in the catnip jar. This will super-charge the toy's attraction to some cats.

Tailoring playtime and exercise routines to match your cat's personality can significantly enhance their quality of life. A one-size-fits-all approach just won't cut it. Each cat needs a bespoke plan, as unique as their whisker patterns or the precise shade of their tortoiseshell coat.

Consider this: If your cat is a high-energy Bengal, incorporating climbing and jumping into playtime will cater to their natural athleticism. On the other hand, a laid-back Persian may enjoy more sedate activities, like interactive puzzle feeders that stimulate their brain without requiring a marathon.

Here is what you can do in order to achieve the goal:

- Observe your cat's responses to different activities. What gets their eyes wide and tail twitching? That's your cue.

- Be flexible and willing to switch things up if something isn't working. Cats can be finicky, and yesterday's hit might be today's miss. Some days your cat might just nope-out on everything.

- Involve all family members in playtime to provide variety and ensure consistency. Different people may bring out different aspects of your cat's playfulness.

Ultimately, catering to your cat's activity level and play preferences promotes both physical and mental stimulation. A well-exercised cat is often a happier, healthier cat. The bonus? You'll likely see fewer midnight zoomies and less property destruction.

Playfulness, or its lack thereof, isn't just an amusing trait; it's a window into your cat's soul. By tuning into their unique personalities and adapting their playtime and activity routines, you're not just meeting their needs—you're deepening your bond. So, grab that feather wand, and let the games begin! Your cat's purrs of contentment will be all the reward you need.

Affection or Aloofness: Decoding Your Cat's Behavior

Understanding why some cats seem distant while others are more affectionate is interesting and reveals a lot about the feline psyche. Let's dive in!

First off, it's essential to recognize that each cat is a unique individual. Just like humans have different personalities, so do cats. Some are naturally affectionate, always ready to snuggle up next to you, while others might be more reserved, preferring solitude to socialization. This variability in affection levels stems from a mix of factors including their personality, upbringing, and past experiences (Foundation, 2013).

Take for example, two cats raised in the same household. One could develop into a lap-loving furball, purring contentedly at every pet, while the other could become an independent explorer, aloof and seemingly uninterested in human interaction. This difference can often be traced back to their early life experiences. Kittens who experience positive human interactions during their formative weeks tend to be more social as adults. Conversely, those who haven't had as much human interaction might be warier.

However, it's not just about their early days. A cat's individual personality plays a significant role as well. For instance, some breeds are known to be more sociable and affectionate, such as the Ragdoll or the Siamese, while others like the Abyssinian may have a more independent streak.

But even within breeds, individual variations exist. So if your tabby prefers quiet corners over cuddles, it doesn't mean they love you any less; they're just expressing their love in their own quirky way.

Speaking of quirks, understanding and respecting your cat's boundaries is vital in fostering trust. Cats are notorious for being creatures of habit and having particular preferences. Have you ever noticed how some cats will recoil from certain types of touch or abruptly walk away during a petting session? That's their way of communicating boundaries. Disregarding these signals can lead to stress and anxiety for your feline friend, potentially damaging your bond.

Here's how you can respect their boundaries to strengthen your connection:

- Observe and learn what types of interactions your cat enjoys. Does she prefer chin scratches over tummy rubs? Pay attention to her cues.

- If your cat moves away or shows signs of discomfort, give her space. Pushing for interaction when she's clearly done can strain your relationship.

- Establish a routine that includes safe, enjoyable interactions, whether it's through play, treats, or gentle petting.

Over time, you'll start to notice subtle changes in behavior that indicate growing trust and affection. It's all about allowing the relationship to develop at your cat's pace, not yours.

Now, let's talk about those affectionate cats—the ones who greet you at the door, follow you around the house, and curl up beside you whenever they get the chance. These cats thrive on regular interaction and positive reinforcement. For example, we brought home littermates and one was very active and loving. He remained underfoot so much, we seriously considered naming him Punt as we accidentally kicked him with what felt like every step. We did not hurt him, but he craved physical contact continuously and did not care that we kept moving and jostling him about.

To keep your affectionate cat happy:

- Engage in daily play sessions. Interactive toys, feather wands, and laser pointers can provide both physical exercise and mental stimulation.

- Offer verbal praise and gentle petting when they seek your attention, reinforcing their affectionate behavior.

- Create a cozy spot where your cat feels comfortable and can relax near you without feeling threatened or smothered.

Cats show affection in many different ways. Some will knead their paws on you, others might give soft headbutts, and some might even bring you 'gifts' in the form of their latest catch. These behaviors are their unique ways of saying "I care about you." Recognizing and responding positively to these gestures can deepen your bond. Your cat may also bring you 'gifts' as they notice you are a terrible hunter and are trying to teach you survival skills.

But what about the cats that seem aloof? According to a study by the Animal Health Foundation, cats can be more responsive to their owner's voice than we often give them credit for

(Foundation, 2013). Their reactions might be subtle—like a slight ear twitch or a brief glance—but it's there. This suggests that even the most seemingly indifferent cats are paying attention and establishing a connection with their humans.

Understanding the cues of affection or aloofness requires patience and observation. Some cats might display affection through indirect actions like staying in the same room with you, following you from a distance, or sitting close but not directly on you. Learning to read these signals can greatly enhance your relationship.

To improve communication with your cat:

- Pay attention to body language. A relaxed posture, slow blinking, and gentle purring are signs of comfort and trust. Tail movements can also be telling; a tail held high is often a sign of a happy cat.

- Use your voice gently. High-pitched, calm tones are usually better received than loud or harsh voices.

- Slow blinking at your cat can mimic their way of showing affection, often referred to as "cat kisses."

Appreciating and accepting your cat's individuality is the cornerstone of building a strong bond. Each cat has its idiosyncrasies and ways of expressing love. By embracing these differences, we can foster deeper connections and ensure our furry companions feel safe, loved, and understood. Whether your cat is a social butterfly or a solitary sphinx, there's a special joy in finding common ground and learning to speak their language, albeit subtly and quietly.

Sometimes, when you're feeling down about your cat's perceived aloofness, remember that the feline-human bond is complex and multifaceted. Much like in human relationships, it requires effort, empathy, and mutual respect. Every ear twitch, every slow blink, and every gentle nudge carries a world of meaning. That's the magic of connecting with cats—they let us into their mysterious world when we least expect it, rewarding our patience and understanding with moments of genuine affection, companionship, and the occasional dead rodent.

Enhancing Your Bond Through Understanding

So, we've dived into the fascinating world of cat personalities and how they influence the way our feline friends interact with us. From social butterflies to introverted mystery-lovers, each cat is an enigma wrapped in fur, claws, and a touch of sass.

Remember earlier when we talked about there being no one-size-fits-all approach to understanding these whiskered wonders? It's crucial to recognize that whether your cat is a high-energy laser chaser or a low-key couch potato, catering to their personality can make your life together much more harmonious. You might have a James Bond-like kitty who enjoys secretive high-jinks or a lounge lizard who prefers to soak up sunbeams without interruption. Embracing your cat's quirks not only makes them happier but also strengthens your bond.

But don't get too comfy just yet—there are a few things you should be mindful of. Ignoring your cat's unique needs isn't just going to lead to a grumpy kitty; it could result in some serious behavioral issues. We're talking shredded curtains, mysterious messes, and those 3 AM house zoomies that make you wonder if you've accidentally adopted a tiny, furry tornado.

On a broader scale, understanding your cat's personality isn't just about keeping your home intact. It's about nurturing a relationship where mutual respect and love flourish. Recognizing that each purr, meow, and headbutt is a form of communication can turn everyday interactions into magical moments. Your aloof kitty isn't ignoring you—they're simply practicing their own brand of feline dignity.

In the end, respecting and celebrating your cat's individuality is the secret sauce for a happy, cohabitant life. Whether they're sneaking behind curtains or demanding belly rubs during your Zoom calls, these weird, quirky, magical beings enrich our lives in ways only a true cat lover can appreciate. So, continue observing, respecting boundaries, and showering affection as needed. After all, isn't that what love—whether human or feline—is all about?

And who knows? Maybe, just maybe, in your cat's eyes, you'll move up from "that person who feeds me" to "the chosen hooman." Now, wouldn't that be something worth purring about?

The Enigmatic World of Cat Dreams

I magine if we could peer into our cats' minds while they snooze, reveal their secret adventures, and share tales of swashbuckling mouse chases or diplomatic flea negotiations. Wouldn't it be amazing if Mr. Whiskers could tell us all about his heroic dreams at the local rodent rodeo? Well, as it turns out, that twitchy whisker dance and those adorable sleep-time murmurs might just be our window into the rich tapestry of their nightly escapades. Welcome to a world where your cat's dreams aren't just cute but full of meaning.

Picture this: you're observing your cat in the middle of a deep slumber. Suddenly, their paws start moving like they're practicing for the next Cat Olympics, and their ears flick as if tuning into an invisible broadcast. These behaviors are more than just amusing—they're clues! Scientists have shown that during REM sleep, the phase when humans dream vividly, cats experience brain activity similar to when they're awake. That moment your furball is pouncing on air? They're likely hunting phantom prey or replaying a favorite bout with their feathery toy. If Fluffy jolts awake, though, she might be battling imaginary enemies or reliving less pleasant memories. Each twitch and turn can tell a tale of instincts and experiences.

In this chapter, we're diving whisker-deep into these feline fantasies to unravel what they reveal about our pets' desires, fears, and interactions. We'll break down common dream motifs, from playful chases to stressful scenarios, and explore ways to engage with your kitty based on their nocturnal narratives. Understanding your cat's dream world can help you create a waking environment that mirrors their secret nighttime adventures, making for a happier, healthier, and more fulfilled furry friend. Get ready to decode the cryptic language of cat dreams and transform tiny twitches into tales worth telling.

Common Dream Activities of Cats

Believe it or not, cats often dream about familiar activities such as hunting, exploring, or interacting with other animals. You might be watching your cat twitch and purr in their sleep and wonder if they're chasing a mouse or exploring uncharted territories – chances are, you're spot on! Remember those moments when your cat pounces on a toy with the precision of a master hunter? They're likely reliving those bursts of excitement during their dreams.

One infamous study involved disabling muscle paralysis in sleeping cats, which led to these kitties physically acting out their dreams – think running in place or swatting at phantom critters (Animals Now, 2023). While these experiments provided insights, it's much kinder (and just as enlightening) to observe our cats naturally. Watching their paws wiggle or their whiskers twitch while they're snoozing gives us glimpses into their secret nocturnal adventures.

As fascinating as this might be, dream motifs in cats can also reflect their deeper instincts, desires, and past interactions. For instance, a kitty dreaming about interacting with other animals might be revisiting memories of a former housemate or encounters with neighborhood cats. Dreams where they exhibit play behavior could signify unmet social needs or pent-up energy that needs releasing.

Moreover, observing a cat's dream motifs can provide insights into their preferences and fears. If you notice your cat frequently jerking awake from what appears to be a nightmare, it might be worth considering if something in their environment is causing them stress or discomfort. Here's what you can do:

- Observe the consistency and context of their dreams. Is there a pattern to when they seem to have more active dreams?

- Provide a comforting and safe environment for them to relax. Ensure their bedding is cozy and located in a peaceful area.

- Use calming products like pheromone diffusers designed specifically for cats, which can help reduce anxiety and promote a sense of security.

Engaging with your cat based on their dream motifs can significantly enhance their mental stimulation and emotional well-being. Imagine transforming your living space into a feline wonderland that mimics their dream adventures! To achieve this:

- Introduce new toys that encourage hunting behavior, such as interactive wands or puzzle feeders.

- Create vertical spaces with shelves or cat trees to fulfill their desire for exploration and climbing.

- Set up a routine playtime session to mimic the playful interactions they might have in their dreams. This not only provides physical exercise but also strengthens your bond with them.

Incorporating these elements into your cat's daily life can turn their dreams into reality, leading to a happier and healthier pet. It's all about understanding their innate behaviors and creating an environment that supports their natural inclinations. Their dreams are telling you what they need – all you have to do is listen and act.

Moreover, let's not forget the importance of variety. Cats, much like us, enjoy new experiences and challenges. Keeping their environment dynamic by rotating toys and adding new elements periodically can keep their minds sharp and prevent boredom. A mentally stimulated cat is a happy cat, and their dreams will thank you for it!

Our cats' dreams are windows into their souls. By understanding and respecting these nocturnal nuances, we can ensure that our feline companions lead enriched lives. The next time you catch your cat in mid-dream, remember – it's not just adorable; it's a clue to what makes them tick. By tuning into these signals, you can make their waking hours as fulfilling as their dreamscape adventures.

Interestingly, the presence of other animals in their dreams—whether it's dogs, birds, or fellow felines—can offer clues about how these creatures impact your pet's waking life. For instance, a dream involving friendly interactions with other cats might signify positive social experiences. On the other hand, an aggressive confrontation could hint at unresolved issues, perhaps with neighborhood felines or even those mischief-filled squirrels that taunt them from trees.

But let's not overlook the symbolic sides either. Dream motifs like encountering specific cat breeds can shed light on your little furball's hidden desires. Take Persian cats, for example. In dreams, they often symbolize comfort and luxury. Maybe your cat yearns for more pampering or thinks it deserves to be treated like royalty! Quite likely since, let's admit, most cats walk around like they own the place (and maybe they do).

Moreover, the color of cats appearing in dreams can also carry significant meanings. Dream interpretations suggest that black cats often symbolize mystery and intuition while white cats may indicate purity or spiritual protection

(Wright, 2024). If your cat dreams of black and white kittens, it could be reflecting its own need for balance or highlighting what's going on in its intricate little head. Some things we may never know.

So, what can these dream signals imply for us, the caring and sometimes perplexed cat parents? Here's a straightforward guide to decode and engage with your cat based on their dream motifs:

- First, observe your cat's behavior closely when they wake up from a seemingly intense dream. Are they curious, playful, or a bit on edge? Their post-dream demeanor is a mini-mystery waiting to be unraveled.

- Next, consider creating a safer environment if you notice signs of stress in their dreams. This might involve enriching their surroundings with more interactive toys or secure hiding spots.

- Engage in activities that align with the dreamy themes. If hunting dominates their dreams, introduce more play sessions with feather wands or laser pointers to satisfy their predatory instincts.

- Lastly, respect their space. If your dream studies point to a need for solitude or independence, allow them those moments. Sometimes, a cozy nook away from the hustle and bustle is all they need.

Engaging with your cat based on dream motifs can truly enhance their mental stimulation and emotional well-being. Offering them outlets that mirror their dream adventures not only keeps them happy but also strengthens your connection. When you cater to their hidden desires and fears, you're acknowledging their complex inner worlds —the ultimate feline appreciation.

In addition to understanding dream behaviors, personal interactions within dreams provide another layer of insights. Playful dreams suggest a happiness and contentment with their environment, urging us to maintain a fun and engaging daily routine. Meanwhile, dreams marked by aggression or fear might signal areas for improvement, indicating possible sources of anxiety in their waking hours that need addressing (Mindberg, 2024).

Imagine if we could ask our cats directly about their dreams! "Mr. Whiskers, did you roll around in an entire field of catnip last night?" Such wishful thinking brings a smile but underlines the essence of our study: caring enough to decode their unspoken thoughts and emotions.

In essence, understanding and supporting your cat's dream life plays a vital role in their holistic well-being. Like humans, cats benefit from emotional recognition and support. So next time you see those cute whisker twitches, remember, you're peeking into a world rich with instincts, desires, and memories, all waiting to be interpreted and nurtured.

Your inquisitiveness about your cat's dream world not only reflects your affection but could pave the way for enriched human-feline relationships. By tuning into these sleepy escapades, we ensure we're responsive to their needs, both seen and unseen. And who knows? With enough practice, interpreting kitty dreams might become your new favorite pastime—adding depth to your already charming companionship.

So, next time your kitty darts awake from another snooze, give him a knowing wink. You've just unraveled another part of his mysterious, dream-filled universe—and isn't that the purr-fect way to show you care?

Insights from Observing Cat Dreams

Dream analysis isn't just for Freud anymore; it applies to our feline friends as well. When you observe these dream scenarios, you might notice recurring themes that hint at what interests your cat most during their waking hours. Is there a particular toy they favor? Or maybe they've developed an aversion to the new vacuum cleaner?

Based on empirical evidence and studies in both human and animal psychology, we know that dreams can reveal latent fears as well. If your cat frequently shows signs of distress—like twitching violently or letting out distressed cries—it might point to underlying anxieties. These could stem from previous negative interactions or situations that caused them stress. It's akin to how certain stimuli can trigger unsettling dreams for us. For instance, Tim Wright's analysis underscores that dreaming about being chased (by another cat, perhaps) often symbolizes underlying tensions

(Wright, 2024). The same principle can apply here.

So, how do you translate these dream observations into practical actions that benefit your cat? Here are some guidelines to consider:

- First, *pay close attention* to physical cues during their sleep. Note any repetitive movements or sounds.

- Second, *keep a dream journal* for your cat. This might sound over the top, but jotting down these details can help spot patterns over time. OK, it is over the top, but after all it is your cat we are taking care of here.

- Third, *create enrichment activities* based on their dream motifs. If your cat dreams of hunting, interactive toys that mimic prey might satisfy this instinct.

- Fourth, *address potential fears* . If you notice any distressing behaviors, try introducing calming elements into their environment, such as soft music or pheromone diffusers.

Understanding your cat's psychological landscape can drastically improve their mental stimulation and emotional well-being. Engaging with your cat based on their dream motifs isn't just whimsical; it can foster a stronger bond between you and your pet. Let's say your cat frequently exhibits playful antics in their dreams. Incorporating more playtime in their daily routine, possibly with new types of toys or even obstacle courses, can keep them mentally and physically sharp.

For example, if jumping on objects seems to be a recurring theme, set up shelves or safe climbing spaces. This satisfies their natural curiosity and adventurous spirit, making their waking hours as fulfilling as their dreams. Conversely, if nightmares are evident, consider creating a safer, more comforting sleeping area. This could involve a cozy bed away from loud noises or disturbances, most likely where kitty cannot even be seen.

Research by Freud suggests that alarming dreams may also indicate an innate resistance to change (Mindberg, 2024). In cats, this might appear as reluctance to explore new environments or unease around unfamiliar objects. Addressing these fears patiently, perhaps by slowly introducing new items or changes in their space, can ease their transitions and promote a sense of security.

Remember that cats are incredibly perceptive creatures. They can pick up on your emotions and reactions too. Keeping a calm demeanor and providing reassurance can go a long way in making them feel safe. If your approach is gentle and consistent, they are likely to mirror that sense of calm back to you.

Moreover, sharing your observations with your veterinarian can provide additional insights. Professionals can offer tailored advice and flag anything out of the ordinary. Your observations can be invaluable for identifying whether there might be underlying health issues affecting their sleep or behavior. Sharing your cat's dream journal with your veterinarian may be received skeptically if they are not familiar with this practice. Again, over the top measures may be appropriate to ensure your best buddy is living the best life possible. When it comes to our fur babies, we can get weird too.

In sum, while it's easy to dismiss the nighttime antics of our feline companions as mere fluff (pun intended), paying closer attention can yield surprisingly significant benefits. From tweaking their environment to enrich their daily lives to addressing deeper anxieties, observing and reacting to your cat's dream world enriches not just their life, but yours as well. It transforms the way you interact with them, deepening your understanding and strengthening the bond you share. So next time your furball is lost in dreamland, take a moment to ponder what adventures they're embarking on—and consider how you can bring a bit of that magic into their waking world.

Engaging with Your Cat Based on Their Dreams

Engaging with your cat based on their dream motifs can enhance their mental stimulation and emotional well-being. Who knew that an afternoon nap for your feline friend might be a window into the intricate labyrinth of their furry minds? Imagining Fluffy chasing invisible mice or exploring uncharted territories in her dreams is amusing, but it's also meaningful. Observing these dream behaviors and responding to them can strengthen your bond and promote your cat's overall happiness. Remember, the aim is not just to tire them out physically but to stimulate them mentally as well.

On those rare occasions when you see contented purring during a cat nap, it's likely your feline friend is having positive interactions in their dreams, possibly recalling affectionate moments or cozy naps in sunbeams. Reinforce this by creating a comforting environment filled with cozy blankets and secure hiding spots. Cats appreciate calm, familiar spaces where they can feel safe and relaxed. Thus, you can influence their dream content indirectly by improving their waking surroundings, planting seeds for pleasant dreamscapes.

If the cat exhibits signs of stress or anxiousness—such as restless sleep or frequent nightmares—it might indicate underlying fears or unresolved past traumas. Identifying and addressing these issues head-on can be transformative.

Here are additional suggestions for what you can do to help:

- Introduce soothing routines, like gentle brushing or soft petting before bedtime.

- Invest in pheromone diffusers to create a calming atmosphere.

- Provide quiet, secluded nooks where your cat can retreat and feel safe.

- Engage in slow, deliberate play to build confidence and trust gradually.

Various dream motifs, like running or fleeing, could imply that your cat has pent-up energy or anxiety. Addressing this through regular, structured playtimes involving puzzles or feeder toys can help alleviate such worries. It's not just about giving them an outlet but also making them work for their rewards, which keeps their minds sharp and engaged.

Moreover, understanding that cultural influences shape our perceptions of cats' behaviors helps nuance our responses to their needs. For example, dream analysis from different cultures reveals that elements like flying or being pursued have diverse meanings (Wright, 2024). Your interpretation of your cat's actions might benefit from considering your own cultural background and experiences with animals.

Pay attention to repetitive actions during sleep, as these may echo particular experiences or desires your cat holds close. Dreams about roaming free in open spaces can suggest a craving for more adventure. Take your cat outside in a secure harness or build a "catio"—a cat patio—to safely explore the outdoors. The new sights, sounds, and smells offer immense enrichment, fulfilling their adventurous spirits without compromising safety.

Engaging with your cat based on their dream motifs isn't as far-fetched as it sounds. It's about creating a reciprocal relationship where you respond to the silent narratives they experience during their sleep. Enhancing mental and emotional well-being goes beyond physical care; it involves recognizing and nurturing their inner lives.

Recent advancements show we can modulate dream experiences using noninvasive methods like transcranial direct current stimulation (tDCS) over sensorimotor areas, demonstrating a reduction in dream movement during REM sleep (Ball et al., 2020). While these techniques are primarily used in research settings, they highlight the importance of the neurological aspects of dreaming. This adds another layer to our understanding and approach to enhancing our pets' lives. We have gone over the top again, but who knew you could influence dreams in this way?

Let's consider the broader implications too. Engaging with your cat on this level by observing its dreams is a celebration of the complex beings they are. You're not only catering to their immediate needs but also acknowledging their subconscious worlds. It's a holistic approach to pet care that enriches both your lives.

In conclusion, by observing and reacting to your cat's dream motifs—a seemingly whimsical endeavor—you unlock deeper avenues for bonding and well-being. Recognize the significance of those twitching paws and softly whimpering snores. They are echoes of your cat's instinctual drives, emotional states, and past interactions.

Living with cats is not merely about cohabitation; it's about understanding and participating in their rich inner worlds. So next time you catch your cat in the throes of an intense nap, remember there's more happening beneath those closed eyelids than meets the eye. Engage with them meaningfully (while they are awake, of course), and you'll find your shared life becoming richer and more rewarding for both.

Well-Being Through Understanding Dreams

As we wrap up this exploration of dream motifs in our feline friends, it's clear that their nocturnal adventures offer us more than just adorable Instagram moments. We've delved into how these dreams can mirror their instincts, desires, and even past interactions. From the twitching whiskers to the phantom paw swipes, your cat's dream life serves as a secret window into their inner world.

Remember when you peeked at your snoozing kitty and wondered if they were off on some grand mouse-chasing expedition or rolling in fields of catnip? Well, turns out they probably are! Whether it's reenacting their most exciting hunts or grappling with imaginary squirrels, these dreams reveal the primal hunter within them. But don't be fooled—these night-time behaviors aren't just cute; they can tell us so much about what makes our cats tick.

On a deeper level, we've seen that dream motifs often reflect your cat's interactions and emotional state. A friendly dream encounter might signal positive social experiences, while an aggressive one could hint at unresolved turf wars with neighborhood felines. And let's not forget those quirky cat breed dreams: if your cat dreams of Persians, maybe she's telling you she deserves more pampering!

So where does that leave us? For the dedicated cat owner, understanding these dreams means creating a living environment that mirrors their dream quests. Imagine morphing your home into a feline funland with interactive toys, inviting climbing spaces, and cozy nooks for those much-needed solitary naps. Not only will this make waking hours more delightful, but it might also lead to sweeter dreams for your furry friend.

However, don't ignore warning signs. If your cat frequently wakes up from what seems like a bad dream, it could indicate stress or anxiety. Make their sleeping area as comforting as possible and consider pheromone diffusers to promote a sense of security. After all, a little kitty reassurance goes a long way.

The broader consequence of all this? By tuning into these subconscious cues, you're not just responding to their needs—you're fostering a deeper bond. This approach transforms pet ownership from mere cohabitation into a connected and fulfilling companionship. It's not just about making them happy but about mutual enrichment and understanding.

So what's next? Keep observing, keep engaging, and who knows? You might just become the Sherlock Holmes of kitty dreams. The next time kitty gives a tiny meow in his sleep, give him a mental high-five. You've unlocked another piece of his tiny mysterious mind.

In closing, remember that every twitch, purr, and paw swipe is a tale waiting to be told. By tuning into these silent stories, you and your furry companion can navigate a world filled with shared adventures and deeper connections. Now, go forth and embrace the whimsical wonders of your cat's dream world!

Nutritional Needs
and Feline Feasts

I magine if your cat had its own chef's hat and a tiny whisk. Now picture the dazzling array of gourmet dishes that whiskered gourmand would demand: delicate slices of tuna tartare, perhaps, or a roasted quail served on a silver platter. Welcome to the culinary universe of cats, where every meal is an opportunity to navigate their exacting tastes and nutritional needs. It's like trying to please Gordon Ramsay—except your critic curls up in your lap afterward.

Cats are obligate carnivores, meaning they need meat to survive and thrive. Unlike us, who can get by on salads and smoothies, our feline friends need animal-based proteins to keep their engines purring smoothly. For instance, taurine, an amino acid found only in meat, is crucial for a cat's heart health and vision. Without it, they could face serious health issues, which means a purely vegetarian diet simply won't cut it. Imagine putting diesel in a car that requires gasoline—not a good idea, right? Similarly, cats need nutrients only found in meat to keep them healthy and full of life.

In this chapter, we're whisking you through the essentials of feline nutrition. We'll explore why a meat-based diet is non-negotiable, delve into specific nutrients like taurine that your cat can't live without, and examine how to satisfy even the fussiest eaters. Ready to become a master chef in your cat's eyes? By the end, you'll be armed with all the knowledge needed to serve up meals that keep your feline friend as healthy as they are happy. Bon appétit!

The Importance of Meat-Based Diets for Cats

Understanding why cats thrive on meat-based diets is pivotal for anyone striving to deepen their relationship with their feline companions. So, let's dive into it!

Cats are obligate carnivores, a fancy way of saying they are genetically designed to thrive on meat. Picture your adorable furball as a lion stalking its prey in the wild—minus the roaring and more of the playful purr. Their bodies are like perfectly tuned machines that run best on animal-based proteins. You cannot fuel a race car with regular gasoline instead of high-octane fuel—it just doesn't work as well. Similarly, cats need nutrients only found in meat to keep their engines running smoothly.

One essential nutrient that meat provides is taurine, an amino acid that's crucial for their overall health. Unlike dogs or humans, cats can't produce enough taurine on their own, no matter how many yoga classes they attend. Taurine supports vital functions like heart health, vision, and digestion. Without enough of it, they could face serious health issues. Think of taurine as that magical ingredient in grandma's famous cookie recipe; without it, those cookies wouldn't be the same—and neither would your cat's health!

In addition to taurine, meat packs a punch of other important nutrients like arginine, fatty acids, vitamins, and minerals that come together to make a wholesome meal for your feline friend. These nutrients contribute to a shiny coat, strong muscles, and a robust immune system. Your cat might not care about winning beauty contests, but looking good often equates to feeling good!

Now, you don't have to take my word for it. Seeking advice from a veterinarian can give you peace of mind and ensure your cat's diet meets all their carnivorous needs. Here's what you can do to get started:

- First, book an appointment with a vet who understands your desire to feed a meat-based diet.

- During the consultation, discuss your cat's current diet and any health concerns you may have.

- Ask for a tailored nutrition plan that includes high-quality meat sources.

- Follow up periodically to adjust the diet as needed, ensuring it continues to meet your cat's needs.

Incorporating high-quality meat-rich foods into your cat's diet is like adding premium ingredients to a homemade dish; it elevates the entire experience. Thankfully, it's easier than ever to find food options specifically designed for the discerning tastes of our feline friends. When choosing food, steer clear of fillers and artificial additives. Here's how you can make sure you're on the right track:

- Look for labels specifying "complete and balanced," which means the food meets nutrient profiles established by organizations like AAFCO.

- Opt for brands that use real meat as the primary ingredient, avoiding those that list vague terms like "meat by-products."

- Consider varying protein sources (chicken, beef, fish) to keep meals interesting and nutritionally diverse.

A key takeaway is that prioritizing a meat-based diet will pave the way for optimal feline health. However, as we've discussed, don't go it alone—consult with a vet for personalized professional nutritional guidance if you choose. This way, you're not just feeding your cat; you're nourishing their body, soul, and maybe even their mischievous spirit.

If you've ever watched your cat leap astonishingly high just to bat at a feather toy, you've witnessed first-hand the energy and agility that a proper diet can support. High-quality proteins play a pivotal role in maintaining that spring in their step—or should I say, leap?

Your kitty's wellbeing isn't just about meeting their dietary needs; it's also about ensuring they live their best life. And let's be honest—when your cat is happy and healthy, everyone benefits. There's less stress, fewer vet bills, and more delightful moments watching your little predator play, explore, and snuggle.

Just remember, every cat is unique, and their dietary preferences can be as quirky as their personalities. While one cat might go bananas for chicken, another might turn up their nose unless it's turkey time. It's all part of their charm. Tailoring your approach based on keen observation and evidence-driven choices can make all the difference.

Navigating the culinary world of your feline friend is akin to being both a chef and a detective. You must suss out their preferences, provide top-quality ingredients, and ensure everything adds up to a complete and balanced diet. Consulting with a vet is like having an expert sous-chef guiding you along the way. And trust me, a vet's guidance can prevent many culinary catastrophes down the line.

So here's to happier, healthier cats! By investing in a meat-based diet tailored to their needs, you're setting the stage for a lifetime of joy-filled cat antics and loving companionship. After all, the secret to a cat's heart really does start with their stomach. Enjoy the journey of discovering what makes your whiskered wonder thrive!

Managing Selective Eating Habits in Cats

Navigating the dietary requirements of our feline friends is like navigating a culinary minefield. Yes, cats can be as picky as that one friend who insists the tomatoes on their pizza are diced and not sliced. When it comes to managing selective eating habits in our cats, though, it's less about fancy preferences and more about ensuring they get the nutrition they need while satisfying their refined tastes.

One effective strategy for addressing finicky eaters is introducing variety in textures and flavors. Just like humans, cats have different taste buds and palate preferences. Some cats might enjoy the meaty texture of shredded chicken, while others might prefer the smoothness of pâté. Experimenting with different options can sometimes feel like playing a game of "Will he eat this?" but can ultimately add excitement to mealtime. Here's what you can do in order to achieve this:

- Try offering different types of cat food – dry kibble, wet canned food, or even semi-moist options. Each has unique textures and moisture content.

- Rotate among various flavors like chicken, fish, beef, and turkey. You never know which one will hit the jackpot for your cat's taste buds.

- Incorporate food toppers or mix-ins such as freeze-dried meat treats or broths to enhance flavor and entice your kitty to dig in.

Another tip is gradually transitioning to new foods to prevent digestive upsets and encourage acceptance. Cats, like many creatures of habit, can be resistant to change. Switching their diet too quickly can result in stomachaches, diarrhea, vomiting, or refusal to eat. Patience here is key.

Here's how to successfully transition their food:

- Start by mixing a small amount of the new food with their current favorite. Gradually increase the proportion of the new food over the course of a week or two.

- Observe but don't rush. If your cat shows signs of digestive distress, slow down the transition to allow their system to adjust.

- Keep mealtimes consistent so your cat becomes familiar with both the routine and the shifting diet.

For those cats who prefer nibbling throughout the day or grazing, rather than feasting in one sitting, offering small, frequent meals could be the answer. This method aligns with a cat's natural hunting instincts, where they would typically catch several small prey in a day. Providing multiple smaller meals can also help regulate their intake and maintain their energy levels.

To create an optimal feeding routine:

- Divide your cat's daily food allowance into several smaller portions and serve these at regular intervals.

- Use timed feeders if you're not able to be home throughout the day, ensuring your cat receives their meals consistently.

- Monitor their intake to ensure they're eating the right amounts without overeating or wasting food.

However, patience and consistency remain vital in addressing selective eating behaviors. Cats aren't born finicky; often, we unintentionally nurture these habits. While addressing their quirks, it's crucial to stay patient and avoid getting frustrated. Consistency in feeding times and methods helps establish a comfortable routine that can ease anxiety around meals.

Experimentation is sometimes necessary. Offer different food options to understand what suits your cat best. Yet, always respect their pace and preferences. Maintain a steady feeding routine and monitor their response to changes. If you notice troubling eating habits—eating too little or acting disinterested even in favorites—it's wise to seek veterinary advice. They can rule out medical issues and provide tailored recommendations (Nutrition, 2017).

When you think about it, catering to a cat's dietary whims is akin to mastering the art of diplomacy. You're balancing your kitty's health needs with their culinary desires, all the while ensuring that mealtimes don't turn into a battlefield. Let's face it, watching a cat turn its nose up at gourmet salmon is both frustrating and laughable.

Consider also the sources of commercial cat food. Dry food tends to be convenient and cost-effective, but it lacks the moisture found in wet options. On the flip side, canned food offers higher palatability and water content, essential for hydration. Cats require a high-protein diet due to their carnivorous nature, so make sure protein tops the ingredient list (n.d., 2017). This approach helps maintain their health while keeping them interested in their meals.

Remember, some cats may develop aversions to certain foods based on prior experiences. Like humans avoiding a dish that once gave them food poisoning, cats can be wary if a specific food coincided with a bad tummy ache. If you suspect this might be the case, try switching to a completely different type of food – maybe even use a new bowl to eliminate any lingering scent memories (Alegría-Morán et al., 2019).

If you've tried all else and still find yourself stuck in the trenches of feline pickiness, seeking professional guidance from your veterinarian can offer new insights and solutions. They can conduct thorough examinations to ensure there aren't underlying health issues affecting your cat's appetite. Additionally, they can recommend specific dietary plans suited to your cat's needs (Nutrition, 2017).

In essence, managing your cat's selective eating habits isn't just about filling their bowls with random assortments of food. It's about crafting a dining experience that resonates with their inherent preferences and health requirements, transforming mealtime from a mundane task into an enriching ritual. So, take a deep breath, embrace the challenge, laugh at the quirks, and enjoy the process of discovering what makes your feline companion purr in contentment with a full belly and overall good health.

Mimicking Natural Hunting Instincts During Feeding

When you think about feeding your cat, you might just picture a bowl of kibble or that gushy, stinky wet food they can't get enough of. But what if I told you that the way you feed your cat could actually help them channel their inner jungle predator and keep them spry and happy? Let's dive into some tactics to mimic your cat's natural hunting instincts during feeding times. Not only will this keep them entertained, but it also benefits their overall health.

First up, interactive feeding toys and puzzles. These are not just fancy gadgets; they are tools that engage your cat's brain and body in food-seeking activities. Cats are natural hunters and crave the mental stimulation that comes with stalking prey. Some cats are naturally food-motivated and meal time is the highlight of their day. Traditional feeding bowls simply don't provide a challenge. Instead, try using treat balls or puzzle feeders.

Here's a quick guide on how to introduce these fun feeding toys:

- Start by placing a few of your cat's favorite treats inside the toy.

- Show your cat how the toy works by playing with it yourself. Roll it around and let the treats fall out.

- Encourage your cat to interact with the toy. You might need to nudge them a little, but curiosity will usually take over.

- Gradually increase the difficulty by adding more treats or using a more complex toy as your cat gets the hang of it.

According to the IAABC Foundation, cats that are mentally stimulated through such activities show less stress and destructive behaviors (IAABC Foundation, n.d.). It's like giving them a little puzzle to solve every time they want to eat—a win-win for both you and your feline friend!

Another effective strategy is scatter feeding or hiding small portions of food around the house. This promotes both physical and mental exercise, transforming meal times into an adventurous scavenger hunt. Imagine your home as the savannah and your cat as a tiny lion on the prowl. They'll have to use their senses to find the hidden morsels, mimicking their natural hunting sequence.

Here's how you can make scatter feeding work:

- Start by hiding bits of dry food or treats in easy-to-find places like under tables or in corners.

- Gradually move to trickier spots, such as behind cushions or on top of cat trees.

- Rotate hiding spots frequently to keep things fresh and exciting for your cat.

Research indicates that this method not only keeps your kitty active but can also prevent obesity and related health issues (Pack, 2019).

Plus, it makes them feel more fulfilled and happy —like they've just caught a mouse!

Next, let's talk about encouraging foraging behaviors through food-dispensing toys. These nifty devices can be filled with kibble or treats, and your cat has to figure out how to retrieve the food. Similar to interactive feeders but often more complex, food-dispensing toys can alleviate boredom and reduce overeating, a common issue among indoor cats who might not get enough exercise.

To get started with food-dispensing toys:

- Begin with simpler toys that require minimal effort to dispense food. Think of these as the training wheels of the foraging world.

- As your cat masters these, step up to more challenging ones that involve rolling, pawing, or even slight lifting actions.

- Ensure the reward distribution is consistent enough to keep your cat engaged without making it too easy.

The Michelson Found Animals Foundation suggests that introducing such complexity in feeding routines can significantly improve a cat's overall behavior and mental state (Animals, 2019). So, the next time your cat seems a bit restless, consider it a cue to bring out a new food-dispensing challenge.

Lastly, incorporating scheduled playtime before meals can simulate a full hunting sequence. Wild cats stalk, chase, and finally capture their prey before they eat. Mimicking this process right before mealtime can help satisfy these deeply ingrained instincts, and best of all, it helps burn off some of that boundless energy.

You can incorporate this idea into your routine by:

- Setting aside 10-15 minutes before each meal for an active play session.
- Use toys that simulate prey movements, like feather wands or laser pointers, to get your cat running, jumping, and pouncing.
- Vary the type and speed of toys to keep your cat guessing and fully engaged.

This pre-meal playtime doesn't just curb pent-up energy; it also primes your cat for digestion and helps create a structured daily routine. According to the IAABC Foundation, allowing cats to engage in predatory play can boost their confidence and happiness (IAABC Foundation, n.d.).

In summary, providing enrichment through feeding challenges, promoting activity through mealtime interactions, and supporting your cat's natural hunting instincts isn't just beneficial—it's necessary for their well-being. By integrating interactive toys, scatter feeding, foraging behaviors, and pre-meal playtime, you're offering your feline friend a richer, more satisfying life.

So, next time you set down that food bowl, think about how you can turn that mundane task into an exciting adventure. Your cat's mind and body will thank you, and you'll likely see a happier, healthier kitty prowling around your home. And remember, a busy cat is a content cat— so let's get those paws moving!

Safe Options for Indulging Your Cat's Palate

When it comes to indulging your cat's palate, the key is finding a balance between giving them delightful treats and ensuring their health remains top priority. After all, our feline friends depend on us to keep them in tip-top shape while satisfying their culinary curiosities.

First, let's delve into some safe treat options for our cats. Research has shown that not all treats are created equal, and it's crucial to choose those that complement your cat's diet without excessive caloric intake. Cats, much like humans, can suffer from overindulgence. Obesity in felines is a growing concern, leading to serious health problems such as diabetes and arthritis. Here is what you can do in order to achieve the goal:

- Check the ingredients list on commercial cat treats, opting for those with high-quality protein sources and minimal fillers.

- Avoid treats containing additives, artificial coloring, or preservatives.

- Ensure that any store-bought treats align with your cat's specific dietary needs—particularly if they have food sensitivities or allergies.

- Remember to consult your veterinarian before introducing new treats to your cat's diet to ensure they're appropriate.

Homemade treats using feline-friendly ingredients offer an excellent, personalized snack alternative. Not only do homemade treats allow you to control what goes into your cat's snacks, but they also provide an opportunity for some fun kitchen bonding time. Many cat lovers find joy in preparing these treats, knowing exactly what wholesome ingredients they're feeding their pets (Animals, 2019).

Here's a simple recipe your cat might enjoy: *mix 10oz. of undrained canned tuna in water, 1 cup whole wheat flour, and 1 egg to create a dough. It will be sticky. Grease a cookie sheet. Shape mixture into little bites and bake at 350F on middle rack of oven for about 20 minutes or until light golden brown and firm.* Voila! A delicious treat your cat will adore! Cats do not digest wheat like we do. It can cause gastrointestinal upset, remember they are meat-eaters after all, so using less flour will make a more digestible treat; however, your mixture will be sticky and difficult to work with as indicated. Adding more flour will firm the dough. Just remember, moderation is key: cats will really enjoy these treats but feed them a few at a time regardless of how much flour you use. Wheat flour is in plenty of other cat food products, making it part of the usual housecat diet. We just want to keep the tummy aches and tuna toots to a minimum. Also putting the tuna in a food processor prior to mixing will result in smoother, more aesthetically pleasing dough, but we can assure your cat will not care, not one bit. You can add flour until the dough is a consistency you can roll out. Roll it flat to 1/4 inch thick and use a small cookie cutter (3/4 inch or smaller) to cut into artisanal shapes if you fancy. Try cutting dough into 1/2 to 1 inch strips, then dicing into cat-bite size triangles. You will end up with a ton of treats. Store baked treats in an air-tight container. They should be good for 14 days stored this way.

However, even as we explore indulgent options for our cats, it's critical to be aware of the limitations on human foods. Certain human foods can be toxic to cats and should be avoided at all costs. *Chocolate, onions, garlic, grapes, and raisins* are among the big no-nos. Furthermore, fatty and salty foods can lead to severe digestive issues or even pancreatitis in cats (The Animal Foundation, 2019). So, no sharing your holiday leftovers unless they're specifically prepared for feline consumption! Cats also do not have a sweet tooth, so high sugar or very sweet treats will not be particularly attractive to them. Think about that lion on the Savannah; it isn't hunting lollypops!

Balancing treat frequency and portion sizes is essential to prevent obesity and promote overall well-being. It can be tempting to shower our cats with snacks every time they look at us with those big, pleading eyes, but moderation is key. Here are some tips to maintain that balance:

- Limit treat-giving to special occasions or as rewards during training sessions. We confess to giving treats just for being cute. It happens. Don't judge.

- Follow the "10% rule": treats should make up no more than 10% of your cat's daily caloric intake.

- Portion out treats into small, bite-sized pieces to avoid overfeeding.

- Opt for low-calorie, nutritionally balanced treats when possible.

The treat recipe above does strike a perfect balance between indulgence and health benefits. For example, these treats can please both dogs and cats. This simple recipe can be made with salmon or tuna mixed with egg and some flour as described above. Once baked, they become crispy delights loaded with omega-3 fatty acids, which are great for maintaining a healthy coat and skin.

In addition to traditional treats, incorporating certain foods into your cat's regular diet can also provide variety and excitement. Small amounts of cooked chicken or turkey, chunks of apple, or pumpkin puree can serve as fantastic supplements. Yes, most cats like pumpkin! Next time you carve one up for a Halloween jack-o-lantern, let your kitty have a sniff of the scooped out inside goop or provide a few chunks of the rind. It might surprise you with a few licks or chomp on the fleshy part of the rind in curiosity. This is a great opportunity for enrichment and mental stimulation. Keep those knives and carving tools stowed safely away before allowing kitty access the pumpkin carving area. If you need moist food in a pinch and have dry kibble on hand, add some plain pumpkin puree. The cat will find this far more palatable than dry food sprinkled with water. Pumpkin puree naturally provides water and fiber to the cat's diet and is a healthy additive. Just remember to keep portions small and introduce new foods gradually.

An important aspect to keep in mind is the role treats play in enrichment for your cat. Besides being tasty morsels, treats can be used in puzzle toys or hidden around the house to encourage natural hunting behavior. This mental stimulation is just as vital for your cat's health as a balanced diet.

Remember, while treats are a wonderful way to express love and reward good behavior, the primary focus should always be your cat's overall health and wellness. Moderation and mindfulness go hand-in-hand here; enjoy the process of creating and sharing treats with your feline friend while keeping their best interests at heart.

To recap: opt for nutritious treats, avoid harmful foods, moderate treat consumption, and prioritize your cat's health in treat choices. Let's strive to make every treat a joyful moment that supports our furry friends' long-term well-being. And always, keep an eye on the evidence and data because the best decisions are informed decisions. Now, go ahead and give your kitty some love—with care and consciousness!

Fostering Healthy and Happy Feline Eating Habits

Navigating the culinary world of your feline friend is akin to being both a chef and a detective. You must suss out their preferences, provide top-quality ingredients, and ensure everything adds up to a complete and balanced diet. Consulting with a vet is like having an expert sous-chef guiding you along the way. And trust me, a vet's guidance can prevent many culinary catastrophes down the line.

In this colorful journey through cat cuisine, we've explored the ins and outs of why cats need meat-based diets and how to manage their selective eating habits. We've also delved into making mealtime exciting by mimicking natural hunting instincts and offering safe treats that cater to their discerning palates. From taurine-packed meats to engaging feeding puzzles, we've gathered tips and tricks to satisfy both your kitty's taste buds and nutritional needs.

Remember that picture I painted at the start? Your home as a savannah, and your cat as a pint-sized lion on the hunt? It's more than just an adorable image—it's a reminder that honoring their natural instincts enriches their lives and strengthens your bond. After all, a well-fed cat is a happy cat, which means fewer hairballs in your shoes and more purr-filled snuggles on the couch.

But let's not forget that every whiskered wonder is unique. While one might leap at the chance for chicken pâté, another might demand gourmet salmon served at precisely 72 degrees Fahrenheit. This quest to understand and cater to your cat's needs is ongoing, and it requires patience, observation, and maybe a few humorous moments along the way—like when your "gourmet" darling decides to eat the same kibble they refused yesterday.

For those worrying about the picky eater who turns their nose up at anything new, take heart. With gradual changes, mixed textures, and the occasional hilarious trial and error, you'll eventually crack the code to their perfect menu. And if all else fails, a little sprinkle of love—and possibly some veterinary advice—can go a long way.

On a broader scale, understanding feline dietary needs helps us appreciate our pets' wild origins and their intricate biology. It teaches us respect for their inherent behaviors and underscores the responsibility we have as their caretakers. The rewards? A thriving cat that leaps, plays, and cuddles with pure joy, enriching your life with their endearing quirks and endless antics.

So, here's to the adventurous spirit of digging deeper into our feline friends' dietary mysteries! Keep experimenting, keep observing, and most importantly, enjoy every moment of your culinary journey together. After all, as much as the secret to a cat's heart starts with their stomach, the joy comes full circle back to you with every contented purr and playful leap. Bon appétit to you and your fur-tastic companion

Cat-Proofing Your Home

A h, the joys of sharing your home with a cat: the love, the purring, the inevitable chaos! Whether it's a leisurely stroll across your laptop during a meeting or a midnight zoomie session that turns your living room into an impromptu race track, cats sure know how to keep life interesting. But amidst all this feline fun lies a sly menace—potential hazards lurking in your home. From toxic plants to chewable electrical cords, these dangers are sneaky adversaries to your floof's well-being. So, let's face it, if your home isn't securely cat-proofed, you might as well be living with a tiny, fluffy daredevil.

Picture this: You've just adorned your windowsill with lush greenery, only to find your kitty sampling each leaf like he's at a botanical buffet. The problem? Some houseplants, such as lilies and philodendrons, can turn your curious kitty's snack time into an emergency vet visit. And let's not forget the excitement of discovering that electrical cords make for thrilling new chew toys, a choice that could tragically zap away nine lives in one go. Or perhaps you've noticed your cat batting around a rubber band, blissfully unaware it's a potential choking hazard. These seemingly innocuous household items are silent stalkers in your pet's playground.

In this chapter, we're diving tail-first into the essential steps for creating a safe and enriching environment for your cat. We'll sniff out the common hazards that could jeopardize your little adventurer's safety and offer up practical advice on mitigating these risks. Whether it's turning your plant collection into a cat-friendly jungle, securing those tempting electrical cords, or ensuring cleaning products are locked away from curious paws, we'll cover it all. By the end of this chapter, you'll be armed with all the knowledge you need to transform your home into a safe haven for your feline overlord, making sure their adventures stay fun—and harmlessly mischievous. Happy cat-proofing!

Safeguarding Your Home Against Common Hazards

Creating a safe and enriching environment for your cat involves identifying and addressing potential hazards that could turn your home into a feline minefield. While balancing personal freedom and social responsibility, one must also consider the welfare of their feline friends. Let's dive into some guidelines and suggestions that will help safeguard your home against common hazards for cats.

Ensuring all houseplants are non-toxic to cats is crucial in preventing accidental ingestion that can harm your feline companion. Cats, as curious creatures, often munch on plants. However, not all greenery is kitty-friendly. Many common houseplants, such as lilies, poinsettias, and philodendrons, can be toxic—even deadly—to cats (Cornell University College of Veterinary Medicine, 2017). So, before you channel your inner botanist and fill your home with flora, cross-check each plant's toxicity levels. Here's what you can do:

- Research and make a list of cat-safe plants. AI has made research simple. You can snap a pic of the plant in question and search if it is cat-safe or not. There is no excuse to poison your bestie with a houseplant!

- Replace any toxic plants with safer alternatives like spider plants or bamboo palms.

- Place plants out of reach or in hanging baskets where adventurous paws can't get to them.

Here's a short list of cat-friendly houseplants: African violet, air plant, bamboo, Boston fern, cast iron plant, Christmas cactus, haworthia, herbs (basil, sage, & thyme), palms (excluding sago palm), phalaenopsis orchids, spider plant, wax plant.

Securing electrical cords and outlets helps protect your cat from potential electrical shocks or injuries from chewing on wires. Picture this: Your playful furball decides an electrical cord is a new chew toy. It's a shocking scenario, literally! Electrical cords pose significant risks, from burns to electrocution. Here's a simple set of actions to take:

- Use cord organizers or wraps to bundle and conceal wires.
- Invest in cord covers that protect both the cables and your cat.
- For added security, unplug devices when they're not in use.

Storing cleaning products and chemicals in secure cabinets ensures your cat doesn't come into contact with harmful substances. Cats have a knack for exploration, and even those tight spaces under the sink aren't safe from their curiosity. It's imperative to keep household cleaners, detergents, and other chemicals securely stored. Products containing bleach, phenols, and other harsh chemicals can cause severe health issues if ingested or inhaled (Rescue, 2023). To keep your regal ruler safe:

- Store cleaning supplies in locked cabinets or high shelves.
- Immediately clean up any spills and thoroughly rinse areas after cleaning.
- Consider using pet-safe cleaning products whenever possible.

Keeping small objects like rubber bands or small toys out of reach helps prevent choking hazards for curious cats. Ever found your cat batting a rubber band across the floor? While it might look innocent, these small objects can be a choking risk. Rubber bands, hair ties, and tiny toys can wreak havoc if swallowed, necessitating costly emergency surgeries (American Veterinary

Medical Association, n.d.). Rubber bands and hair ties with elastic or rubberized insides can cause obstructions in the digestive system; they can wrap around the intestines and stop everything from moving. This presents an emergency since everything is blocked/obstructed and will be fatal if not removed immediately. Not only is the risk of obstruction like this potentially lethal, it is also very expensive to treat and complicated. So, while it is amusing to play with rubber bands and hair ties, it is an extremely bad idea. Keep them away from your kitty! Here are a few habits to adopt:

- Regularly sweep your floor for tiny objects.
- Store small items in closed containers or drawers.
- Provide safe, appropriate toys for your cat's amusement.

It's essential to regularly inspect your home for potential dangers. Prioritize creating cat-safe environments and always keep emergency contact information for veterinary care easily accessible. We all know how fast felines can teleport from one spot to another; those nimble legs can carry them into hazardous situations in no time. A proactive approach ensures you stay a step ahead, mitigating risks before they become problems.

Addressing these household hazards doesn't just protect our furry pals—it enriches their lives, offering them safe spaces to explore and play.

In summary:

- Always be mindful of the plants you bring into your home.
- Take special measures to childproof electrical setups.

- Ensure all chemicals are stored securely and safely.
- Keep small, potentially hazardous objects well out of reach.
- Regular home inspections and keeping vet contacts handy can avert crises before they spiral.

By applying these practical steps, you'll create an enriching, safe haven for your cat, balancing their natural curiosity with the necessary precautions to uphold their health and safety. After all, a happy, healthy cat makes for a joyful, peaceful home—something we can all stand behind, both personally and socially.

Enhancing Vertical Climbing Opportunities

Providing tall cat trees or shelves allows your cat to engage in natural climbing behavior, promoting physical activity and mental stimulation. Our feline friends are naturally inclined to leap, climb, and perch — behaviors inherited from their wild ancestors who needed to escape predators and survey their terrain. Without these outlets, indoor cats can become lethargic or bored, leading to potential behavioral issues or health problems. You don't need to overthink it; just think of it as giving your kitty a stairway to heaven!

Here's what you can do to achieve this:

- Opt for tall cat trees with multiple levels. These not only provide physical exercise but also serve as a playground that stimulates their minds.

- Consider installing wall-mounted shelves. Start low and gradually increase the height. This creates an exciting path for your cat to explore.

- Ensure stability. Wobbly structures can deter your cat from using them, or worse, cause injury.

- Place treats or toys on different levels to encourage your cat to investigate and climb.

Incorporating scratching posts or pads helps satisfy your cat's need to scratch and stretch, reducing furniture damage and promoting healthy claws. Cats don't scratch to be pesky; it's a crucial part of maintaining their claws and muscles. They also use scratching to mark their territory, both visually and with scent glands located in their paws.

To ensure your cat has ample opportunity to scratch (and save your sofa):

- Provide various scratching surfaces like sisal rope-wrapped posts, cardboard pads, or even mats. Each cat has its preference, so offer a smorgasbord.

- Place scratching posts near where they love to scratch already – maybe beside the armrest of your now-battered couch.

- Vertical and horizontal options cater to different scratching styles. Some cats like to stretch tall and scratch up high, while others prefer scratching flat.

- Rub some catnip on the posts to make them irresistible. Think of it as luring them to the "right" places to scratch.

Creating elevated resting spots encourages your cat to perch (remember the loaf?) and observe their surroundings, offering a sense of security and territory. Cats feel most secure when they can see everything from a vantage point. Those elevated spots aren't just real estate; they're VIP suites where your cat feels like royalty overseeing their kingdom. It's also a safe retreat from potential stressors, like new pets or boisterous guests.

To create these serene sanctuaries:

- Install cozy perches or hammocks near windows where they can bask in the sunlight and watch the world go by. It's like their very own nature documentary on cat-t.v.

- Position shelves at different heights to give your cat plenty of choices. Cats love having options.

- Add soft mats or cushions to these spots for added comfort. Remember, style isn't just for humans; your cat will absolutely appreciate a chic yet comfy retreat.

- Climbing vines or plant holders can blend functionality with aesthetics, making your living space look lush while keeping your kitty happy.

Introducing vertical spaces can help multi-cat households establish territories and reduce conflicts over space. If you have more than one cat, you know how quickly fur can fly if they don't have enough room to claim as their own. Providing elevated zones allows them to stake out personal space without encroaching on each other's turf.

To minimize kitty disputes:

- Allocate separate vertical spots for each cat to claim. This could mean multiple cat trees, shelves, or perches spread around your home.

- Observe your cats' interactions. You might find one cat prefers heights while another is content on a lower level.

- Make sure each key area (like food, water, and litter boxes) has unobstructed access paths through these vertical spaces. Cats can become territorial over essential resources, so avoiding bottlenecks can help keep the peace.

- Monitor usage and adjust placements as necessary. Cats are dynamic creatures, and their preferences can change, especially when new members join the household.

Vertical structures are essential for cats' physical and mental well-being, provide a sense of security and territory, and contribute to a harmonious living environment for multiple cats. By thoughtfully integrating these elements into your home, you're ensuring your feline companions stay active, happy, and stress-free. Plus, let's face it, watching a cat navigate an indoor jungle gym is sheer entertainment gold!

When designing your cat's vertical paradise, you'll be surprised how effortlessly it integrates into your decor. From sleek modern shelves to rustic tree-like structures, there are endless options to suit your aesthetic. Just think of it as framing pieces of art – only this art purrs and occasionally knocks over a plant.

Ultimately, the goal is to enrich your cat's habitat and deepen your bond with them. Happy cats make for happy owners, and creating these climbing opportunities is a significant step toward a thriving, contented feline. So, go ahead and elevate your cat's world; they'll repay you with purrs, headbutts, and possibly fewer shredded curtains.

Maintaining a Clean and Inviting Litter Box

Maintaining a clean and inviting litter box is paramount to creating a safe and enriching environment for your cat. A well-maintained litter box can mean the difference between a happy, well-adjusted feline companion and one that decides your favorite rug is the perfect place to do their business.

First of all, let's talk about the importance of scooping. Every single day, you should scoop out the litter box. Imagine it like this: You wouldn't want to use a toilet that hadn't been flushed in days, right? The same goes for your cat. Daily scooping helps prevent odors and maintains cleanliness. Your cat, with their incredibly sensitive nose, will appreciate a fresh litter box.

Plus, this routine cleanup encourages your cat to consistently use the designated area rather than seeking out less desirable spots in your home (The Humane Society of the United States, n.d.).

Here's what you can do:

- Scoop the litter box at least once daily.
- Make sure to remove any waste clumps and dispose of them properly.
- Using a scoop designed for litter boxes can make this task quick and efficient.

Speaking of litter, not all litters are created equal. Many owners mistakenly believe that cats prefer scented litters to mask odors. However, most cats find scented litters off-putting and may avoid using the box altogether if they find the smell unpleasant (The Humane Society of the United States, n.d.). Opt for unscented litter and ensure that the box has an adequate depth of a few inches. This allows your cat to have enough material to dig and cover their waste, catering to their natural instincts.

Here's how to achieve this:

- Choose an unscented, fine-granule litter that's easy on your cat's paws.
- Maintain a litter depth of about 2-3 inches.
- Monitor the litter levels and add more as needed to keep it consistent.

Location, location, location! Placing litter boxes in quiet, easily accessible locations throughout your home is key. Cats are private creatures who prefer to do their business in peace, away from the hustle and bustle. It's essential to place the litter box in a spot where your cat feels safe but also somewhere that's convenient for them to reach. If you have multiple cats, this is even more critical. Having several boxes scattered around different parts of the house ensures no cat feels cornered or bullied out of using the facilities. According to Maddie's Fund, you'll want one litter box per cat plus one extra, and these should be placed in various rooms (Maddie's Fund, n.d.).

To successfully plan the placement:

- Avoid noisy or high-traffic areas like next to the washing machine or in the living room.

- Ensure there's at least one litter box on each level of your home.

- Place litter boxes in corners or against walls where your cat can see potential intruders and feel secure.

Now, let's dive into the nitty-gritty details of changing and cleaning the litter box. Regularly changing the entire contents of the litter box and giving it a good scrub prevents bacterial buildup and keeps the environment hygienic for your cat. This means completely emptying the box at least once a week, washing it with mild dishwashing liquid, rinsing it thoroughly, and then refilling it with fresh litter (Maddie's Fund, n.d.). Harsh chemicals can deter your cat from using the box, so stick to gentle cleaners.

Follow these steps to maintain cleanliness:

- Weekly, empty the entire litter box and wash it with warm water and mild detergent.

- Rinse thoroughly to remove any soap residue.

- Dry the box completely before adding fresh litter.

Proper litter box maintenance isn't just about preventing unpleasant smells; it's also crucial for your cat's health and well-being. Neglecting the litter box can lead to behavioral issues, where a frustrated cat might decide to relieve themselves elsewhere. Cleanliness is crucial, especially for multi-cat households, where the competition for a clean spot can be fierce (The Humane Society of the United States, n.d.).

Highly scented litter additives may also be offensive to your cat's sensitive sense of smell. Think of walking behind or worse, getting stuck in an elevator with a person bathed in perfume. The fragrance might be pleasant, but too much of it in a confined space might cause a litter box objection. Try unscented baking soda first then use the scented additives judiciously. This will absorb unpleasant odor, allow the pleasant scent to remain, but keep the litter box tolerable to the cat and prolong the usable life span of the litter. The powdery dust will also get stuck to your kitty's paws, so keep it to a minimum as nobody likes to lick perfume and powder, cat nor human.

So, let's encapsulate the key takeaways here. Maintaining a clean and inviting litter box involves several important practices: daily scooping to prevent odors and maintain cleanliness, using fresh litter and ensuring proper depth for comfort, and ability to dig and bury waste, strategically placing litter boxes in quiet and accessible locations, and regular changing and thorough cleaning to prevent bacterial growth. By following these guidelines, you're not only promoting consistent litter box usage but also contributing significantly to the overall health and happiness of your feline friend.

Remember, a little effort in maintaining their bathroom can go a long way in keeping your cat content and your home fresh. And isn't that what we all want? Happy cat, happy life!

Litter boxes are (ick!) the worst part of being a cat parent, but starting with good habits encourages good habits, so set your standard high and do your best to maintain it. The "automatic" or self-cleaning litter boxes are convenient, but you should thoroughly research one before making the investment. Not only are they more costly to purchase but they are not maintenance free and some require specific litter, take up more space, and need more complicated cleaning.

Cats instinctively bury their waste, so don't let anyone tell you they "litter trained" their cat. The cat will literally seek out the best area to do their business. Just show them the litter box and they will use it. If they do not, there are other factors at play: the location, the smell, the texture, or a problem your vet may address. It is, thankfully, an instinctual drive cats have because they do not want to be tracked by any other predator.

Designing Spaces Tailored to Cat Comfort

Designing spaces tailored to your cat's comfort and enjoyment involves a dash of creativity, a sprinkle of love, and a whole lot of observation. Yep, that again. Observation is key in understanding your cat. When setting up your home for your feline friend, think of it as creating a haven where they can be their quirky, curious selves. Let's dive into some practical, yet fun, ways to enhance your cat's environment.

First off, providing cozy beds or blankets in quiet areas gives your cat a safe and comfortable space to rest undisturbed. Just like us, our furry friends need their version of a spa retreat. A quiet corner with a plush bed or a fluffy blanket does the trick. Cats cherish these spots because they're undisturbed by the hustle and bustle of daily life— think of it as their very own "do not disturb" zone. To get started:

- Find a small nook in a low-traffic area of your home.

- Lay down a soft blanket or a cat bed.

- Ensure the spot is away from noisy appliances or air vents.

- Add a familiar toy or item that carries your scent for extra comfort.

Next, incorporating interactive toys and puzzle feeders encourages mental stimulation and physical activity, preventing boredom and excessive energy. If you've ever had a cat zip past you in a blur of fur and claws at 3 AM, you know they have a reservoir of playful energy. Channeling this energy effectively can save your sofa and curtains from becoming impromptu scratching posts. Here's how you can keep your kitty entertained:

- Scatter a variety of toys around the house: feather wands, crinkle balls, and spring toys work wonders.

- Introduce puzzle feeders for meal times. These come in many forms, such as mazes or treat-dispensing balls.

- Rotate toys every few days to maintain their novelty.

- Engage in daily play sessions with your cat using interactive toys. This not only tires them out but strengthens your bond too.

Creating window perches or outdoor enclosures allows your cat to observe nature and engage with the outside world safely. Cats are natural-born spectators. They love watching birds flutter by, leaves rustling, and people walking their dogs—all from the safety of their domain. Setting up a place for them to indulge in their voyeuristic tendencies is both enriching and entertaining. To enrich your cat's view:

- Install a sturdy window perch or shelf.

- Place a soft blanket on the perch to make it inviting.

- Remove any obstacles blocking the window to give them an unobstructed view.

- Consider adding bird feeders outside the window to attract feathered guests.

- For those willing to go the extra mile, set up a "catio" (an enclosed outdoor patio) where your cat can safely enjoy the outdoors.

Offering hiding spots and vertical retreats provides your cat with options to escape and relax in times of stress or anxiety. Think about those moments when unexpected visitors knock on your door or chaos ensues during spring cleaning. Cats, being the introverts they are, appreciate personal spaces where they can retreat and feel secure. Here's how you can create these escapes:

- Provide various hiding spots like small tents or covered beds.

- Arrange vertical spaces such as cat trees, shelves, or wall-mounted perches.

- Ensure these areas are spread throughout the home so your cat always has a safe place nearby.

- Combine hiding spots with vertical spaces to cater to their climbing instincts and need for security on higher ground.

These thoughtful touches don't just make your home more cat-friendly—they also help foster a deeper understanding of your cat's preferences and quirks. Enriched environments promote well-being and happiness, which, in turn, strengthens the bond between you and your feline companion.

To wrap up, designing a cat-friendly space involves a blend of providing cozy nooks, mentally stimulating activities, engaging views, and safe retreats. Each element caters to a different aspect of your cat's nature, ensuring they live a balanced and happy life. Remember, the key is observation and adaptation. What works for one cat might not work for another, so be patient and test various setups to see what brings out the purrs of contentment from your furry friend.

Wrapping Up: Crafting a Safe and Happy Home for Your Cat

As we've journeyed through identifying and addressing potential cat hazards in your home, it's clear that our whiskered friends need both safety and enrichment. Remember, our goal isn't just to wrap our homes in bubble wrap but to create a space where our feline companions can thrive, explore, and be their quirky selves without landing in hot water—or chewing on electrical cords.

We kicked off by talking about those innocent-looking houseplants that could potentially turn into a cat's toxic snack. We followed up with tips on securing electrical cords because, let's face it, nobody wants their cat channeling their inner electrician. The importance of safely storing chemicals and cleaning up spills was next, a step critical for keeping Kitty from becoming an accidental chemist. Then we tackled the tiny choking hazards that might lurk in shadowy corners, proving that regular clean-ups aren't just for spring anymore.

Ultimately, creating a safe and enriching environment boils down to being proactive and perceptive about what could trip up your curious kitty. It's not only about safeguarding your home but enriching your feline friend's life. Address these hazards now, and you'll build a playground where your cat feels both secure and stimulated.

Of course, transforming your home into a cat haven doesn't just benefit your kitty; it positively impacts your own peace of mind as well. By addressing these hazards today, you pave the way for fewer emergencies tomorrow. And let's be real, the less you spend on unexpected vet visits, the more you can invest in extravagant cat trees or that quirky catnip toy you've been eyeing.

So as you ready your toolkit of cord wraps, non-toxic plants, and rubber band collection bins, remember: this isn't just about protection—it's about making your cat's world a joyful and curious place. By creating a safe, delightful environment, you'll not only ensure your kitty stays out of harm's way but also foster a richer, deeper bond with them.

In essence, a harmonious home starts with mindful modifications that cater to your cat's natural instincts while eliminating risks. Who knows? You might even start seeing your living room from a whole new perspective—a cat's-eye view, if you will. Now, on to the next adventure in kitty-proofing! Happy tails await.

Cultivating a Deep Connection with Your Cat

E ver hear the phrase, "cats are like potato chips; you can't have just one"? Well, if we're honest, they're more like those fancy artisanal chips—delicate, layered, and worth savoring. Cats may be easily misunderstood as aloof creatures, but beneath their serene exteriors lies a complex world of emotions and bonds waiting to be nurtured. So, how do you turn your living room into a sanctuary where both you and your cat can achieve zen-like tranquility? It's simpler than assembling that IKEA bookshelf currently lurking in your hallway. This chapter will guide you through creating peaceful, bonding moments that'll make you and your feline BFF closer than ever.

Now, I know what you're thinking: "Why do I need to create tranquil spaces when my cat already has 136 hiding spots?" But think about it— have you ever tried to bond with someone while they're squeezed behind the fridge or under the bed? Not exactly conducive to quality time, right? Cats, much like us, need environments where they feel secure to truly open up. Research shows that creating these safe havens within your home helps build trust and emotional connections. Imagine turning that corner of your small bedroom or bathroom into a comfort zone for your cat, filled with just the right amount of cozy nooks and soft whispers of peace. No renovations required, just a bit of thoughtfulness and some strategic placement of boxes and blankets.

In this chapter, we'll delve into the simple yet effective ways to transform any space in your home into a cat-friendly retreat. From setting up comfortable hideaways to engaging in quiet activities that promote mindfulness, you'll discover practical steps to enhance your relationship with your cat. We'll explore how gentle petting, calm voices, and shared silences can become the foundation of your bond. By the end of this journey, you'll not only understand your cat better but also foster a deeper, more meaningful connection. Ready to unlock the secrets to your cat's heart? Let's dive in!

Tranquil Spaces for Bonding

Creating tranquil and undisturbed spaces for quiet bonding moments allows you and your cat to establish a peaceful connection based on mutual respect and trust. Now, I know it might sound a bit ethereal, but research shows that providing such environments can make a world of difference for both you and your feline friend.

Consider the advice from the San Diego Humane Society—the kindest thing you can do when bringing your cat into a new home is to provide a safe, quiet space where they can adjust gradually (San Diego Humane Society, 2022). This principle doesn't just apply to new homes; it's about creating ongoing safe havens within your home where you and your cat can retreat from the hustle and bustle.

Creating these sanctuaries doesn't require a renovation project. In fact, it's much simpler than that:

- Find a small, quiet corner of your home. Something like a bathroom or small bedroom works wonders.

- Ensure the space is free from built-in hiding places where you'd have to pull your cat out to interact with them. That's more stressful for everyone involved.

- Set up an appropriate hiding spot: Think of an open carrier or a box lined with a towel. Cats love to feel snug and secure.

- Keep their essentials—food, water, bedding—at one end of the room, and their litter box as far away as possible. Cleanliness matters!

- Provide some simple toys. These don't need to be fancy—sometimes a ball of yarn or a feather wand can be exceedingly entertaining.

When you create this environment, you'll likely find your cat feeling safer and more willing to engage in those precious bonding moments. It's not just about making your cat comfortable; it's about building a mutual sanctuary where both of you can decompress and connect.

Quiet interactions such as gentle petting, soft-spoken words, and shared silence promote a sense of tranquility and emotional closeness, strengthening the bond between you and your cat. Imagine sitting in your favorite reading chair with your cat curled up beside you. It's a shared moment of silent contentment—a purr-fect way to fortify your connection.

But how exactly do you engage in this?

- Start by allowing your cat to come to you. Sit quietly in the designated safe space and let curiosity do its work.

- When your cat approaches, extend your hand slowly. Let them sniff and acclimate to your presence.

- If they seem comfortable, start with gentle face pets. Little scratches behind the ears can go a long way.

- Use a calm, soothing voice to talk to your cat. Narrating your day in a soft tone can be surprisingly effective.

- Bring treats as a peace offering. This not only makes them happy but also associates your voice and presence with good things, enhancing the bond.

- Don't rush or force the interaction. Give your cat frequent breaks to explore the space and come back to you when they're ready.

Keep in mind that each cat has their own comfort zone—a space within which they feel safe and loved. By respecting this and following their lead, you'll cultivate a strong sense of trust and attachment.

Engaging in mindfulness practices during quiet moments with your cat fosters a deeper understanding of their needs, emotions, and unique personality traits, enhancing the quality of your relationship. Yes, cats are mysterious creatures, but spending mindful time with them can unravel some of that mystery.

To achieve this,

- Focus on being present in the moment. Put away your phone, turn off the TV, and just be there with your cat.

- Observe your cat's behavior without judgment. Notice whether they are relaxed or tense, playful, or subdued.

- Engage in activities that encourage mindfulness for both of you. This could be slow, rhythmic petting or simply sitting quietly while your cat naps next to you.

- Practice deep breathing exercises. Your calm demeanor will reflect onto your cat, creating a serene bubble for both.

- Listen to the ambient sounds together. The rustling leaves, the hum of distant traffic, or the soft patter of rain can create a soothing backdrop for your time together.

Taking time to appreciate their presence is rewarding in itself. Cats are sensitive animals who pick up on our energy, so the more at peace you are, the more at peace they will be.

Ultimately, it's about recognizing the importance of these quiet moments. They may seem small, almost insignificant, but they weave the fabric of a loving and trusting relationship. Your cat doesn't need grand gestures; they thrive on consistency, security, and the quiet affirmation that comes from simply being together.

In this busy world, taking a few moments each day for some uninterrupted quality time with your cat can make a significant impact. You'll find not only your bond deepening but also a profound sense of companionship that transcends the usual owner-pet dynamic. And honestly, who couldn't use a little more calmness and connection in their life?

So, find that tranquil corner, sit down with your furry friend, and let the silent language of love do the talking. Your cat will thank you in purrs and cuddles, and those shared peaceful moments will become some of the most cherished times you spend together.

The Importance of Shared Peace and Understanding

Creating those small, serene havens isn't just about giving your cat a cushy spot to lounge. No, no—it's like building a gateway to their heart, one small nook at a time. We've discussed how to craft these tranquil spaces with ease—no renovation crews required! Just a corner, some blankets, and maybe a ball of yarn or a cardboard box. This isn't rocket science; it's more like kitty feng shui.

Remember what the San Diego Humane Society said? The best way to welcome a new cat is by offering them a calm space to adjust. But let's extend that wisdom to everyday life because, honestly, who doesn't need a little tranquility amidst the chaos? Think of it as hitting the reset button for both you and your feline friend.

So here we are, advocating for simplicity. It's not just about making your cat comfy but about creating a mutual sanctuary—a place where you can both escape from the wild world beyond your front porch. Here's my stance: More cuddle corners equal happier cats (and humans).

Now, let's get real for a moment. Some skeptics might argue that cats are aloof creatures who couldn't care less about your efforts. But I'll counter with this—ever seen a cat snub a perfectly good cardboard box after initial suspicion? They may play hard-to-get, but deep down, they crave comfort and consistency.

And consider the grander scheme of things. When you create these peaceful spaces, you inadvertently foster a home environment brimming with trust and emotional availability. Imagine a household where random zoomies are complemented by meditative purring sessions. That's balance, my friends.

At the end of the day, these serene moments don't just deepen your bond—they redefine it. You transition from being a mere food dispenser to becoming a cherished companion in their diary of nine lives. As the hustle and bustle of everyday living continues, remember to carve out that quiet corner. Sit down with your furry muse and let the silent conversation flow. Their purrs will be louder than words, and believe me, those cuddly moments will become your most treasured memories.

So go on, find that perfect spot, settle in, and let the magic happen. Your cat will thank you with purrs, head bumps, and perhaps a little less disdain when you accidentally step on their tail. After all, in the tranquil silence of mutual understanding, even the smallest gesture speaks volumes. And who couldn't use a bit of peace and understanding in their life?

Cat Health and Well-Being Essentials

I magine a day in the life of your feline friend: rolling around lazily in sunbeams, expertly stalking imaginary mice, and occasionally gracing you with their royal presence. Sounds like a purr-fect existence, doesn't it? But beneath that seemingly carefree exterior lies a whole world of health concerns waiting to be addressed. Despite their nonchalant demeanor, your cat's well-being is a delicate balance that requires constant attention and care. And no, we're not just talking about keeping their food bowl filled and sharing the occasional cuddle.

Here's the scoop: cats are masters at hiding illness. They could teach courses on being stealthy spies! Imagine Sherlock Holmes with whiskers— they'll give him a run for his money. This means your beloved kitty might continue lounging on his favorite perch, mask firmly in place, even as a health issue silently stalks him. Little changes, like altered eating habits, unexplained weight shifts, or sudden laziness, might seem trivial at first but can hint at deeper problems. Without regular veterinary check-ups, these stealthy issues can escalate, turning minor hiccups into full-blown catastrophes. We wouldn't want our furballs turning into drama queens over something preventable now, would we?

In this chapter, we'll explore the essentials of ensuring your cat's health and well-being. From the importance of routine vet visits and preventive care to understanding age and breed-specific needs, we've got all paws covered. You'll discover tips to make vet trips less traumatic (for both you and your cat) and practical advice on maintaining preventive treatments to keep those pesky fleas and heartworms at bay. Dive into the world of feline grooming practices and dietary considerations, all tailored to navigate the quirks and mysteries of your furry companion. Get ready to embark on a journey that promises to transform you into the ultimate cat guardian, equipped to ensure those nine lives are lived to the fullest!

The Importance of Routine Veterinary Care

Imagine you're a cat. You spend your day lounging on the windowsill, watching birds, or maybe plotting how to stealthily knock that potted plant off the shelf. Life seems perfect—except for those dreaded trips to the vet. Your human insists these visits are necessary, and they're right.

Regular veterinary check-ups are like an all-you-can-eat buffet of health benefits for your feline companion, though perhaps less appetizing than a dish of fresh tuna.

First off, let's dive into why regular check-ups are so crucial. Cats are notorious for being masters of disguise when it comes to illness. They can be the James Bond of hiding symptoms, meaning that, as much as you love and observe them, it's easy to miss early signs of health issues. Regular vet visits allow trained professionals to spot problems before they become big, ugly monsters under the bed (AAHA, n.d.). During these visits, vets perform wellness exams that cover everything from ears to tails. Think of it as a comprehensive audit of your cat's well-being. The goal is to catch any subtle signs of trouble, like heart murmurs or dental issues, long before they start causing distress.

Now, let's talk about preventive treatments. No one enjoys dealing with fleas, ticks, or worse—heartworms. These little critters can turn your cat's life into a nightmare faster than you can say "Meow!" Preventive medications prescribed by your vet can safeguard against these common ailments, ensuring your cat remains comfortable and healthy (Animal Humane Society, n.d.). Vaccinations are another cornerstone of preventive care, protecting your feline friend from potentially fatal diseases like rabies and panleukopenia. It's akin to putting a suit of armor on your pet, allowing them to bravely face the world, even if their main battle involves chasing laser pointers.

Establishing a trusting relationship with your cat's vet isn't just beneficial for health reasons—it also makes those vet visits far less stressful for everyone involved. Here's what you can do to build that trust:

- Make the carrier a familiar and cozy space. Leave it out in the living area so your cat doesn't associate it solely with vet visits.

- Bring along some of your cat's favorite treats or toys. In the cat world, bribery works wonders. We have done some amazing things using those packets of lickable puree.

- Stay calm yourself. Cats are incredibly intuitive and pick up on your stress levels. If you're cool as a cucumber, they'll be more likely to follow your lead.

- Reward your cat post-visit. A tasty treat or extra cuddle time can go a long way in creating positive associations with the vet.

By following these guidelines, you'll help make each exam a breeze, transforming the dreaded vet trip into just another part of your routine. Most cats will shed a bit of hair due to stress. In the wild, this reaction could potentially allow them to slip through the grasp of a foe; on your lap, not so much. Use the grooming or clean up time to praise good behavior or reassure the cat that went bat-crap crazy everything is alright and they are safely in your care.

Understanding the specific needs of your cat's age and breed is another critical element of maintaining their health. Kittens, adult cats, and senior cats all have different requirements, much like how a teenager's diet is different from that of an elderly person. For example, kittens require vaccinations in their first few months to protect against myriad diseases, while senior cats might need more frequent check-ups to monitor age-related conditions like arthritis or kidney disease (Syndram, 2023).

To tailor preventive care measures effectively:

- Talk to your vet about the unique needs related to your cat's breed. Some breeds are predisposed to certain health issues. Knowing this can help you take preventative actions.

- Make adjustments based on your cat's age. Younger cats may need more vaccinations and parasite control, while older cats might benefit from specialized diets and mobility aids, like those little pet stairs to get to their favorite spot without having to make a painful leap.

- Monitor changes in behavior or physical condition. Weight gain or loss, changes in appetite, or energy levels can be significant indicators that your vet should know about.

In essence, understanding your cat's individual needs and making informed decisions can lead to a healthier, happier life for your furry friend.

Incorporating these practices into your routine not only safeguards your cat's health but also strengthens your bond. When you take proactive steps towards ensuring their well-being, your cat senses the care and love behind your actions. This mutual trust and affection give you both more quality time together, free from the shadow of potential health woes.

So, to sum it all up:

Regular veterinary care is fundamental for early detection of health issues, preventing ailments, and easing the stress of vet visits through familiarity and trust. Tackling health proactively will keep those nine lives running smoothly, while understanding and addressing age and breed-specific needs ensures tailored, effective care. Regular check-ups lay a robust foundation for your cat's well-being, enabling you to address health concerns before they escalate.

At the end of the day, remember that your cat relies on you for more than just chin scratches and food. Their health is in your hands, and with the right approach, you can ensure they lead a vibrant, purr-filled life. Picture your cat stretching in a sunbeam, eyes half-closed, content because they feel good. That's the true reward of diligent veterinary care: a happy, healthy companion whose antics continue to amuse and warm your heart for years to come.

Let's make every purr count. After all, in the grand scheme of things, what could be more rewarding than knowing you've done everything possible to give your best friend the full, joyous life they deserve?

Essential Feline Grooming Practices

Regular grooming sessions help prevent matting, hairballs, and skin issues in cats. Cats are meticulous groomers by nature, spending a significant part of their day keeping themselves tidy. But despite their best efforts, cats can still benefit immensely from a little human intervention. Grooming isn't just about aesthetics; it's essential for their health.

Here's what you can do to keep those furballs at bay:

- First, make it a habit to comb through your cat's fur regularly. For short-haired cats, weekly sessions might suffice, but long-haired breeds may need more frequent attention.

- Use a metal comb to work through any knots or mats gently. If you encounter stubborn tangles, try using a detangling spray formulated for pets.

- Brushing their coat helps remove loose hair, preventing the ingestion of hair that could turn into pesky hairballs later on.

- Look out for fleas, ticks, or skin abnormalities such as redness or bumps during these grooming sessions. Early detection can save your kitty from a world of discomfort and potential health issues.

Brushing your cat's coat not only helps distribute natural oils but also strengthens your bond with your feline friend. There's something profoundly calming about a mutual grooming session, where both you and your cat feel productive and content. The act of brushing mimics the sensation they get from licking themselves and others, signaling comfort and affection.

To make this a rewarding experience:

- Choose a time when your cat is naturally relaxed, perhaps after a hearty meal or post-playtime. An anxious or energetic cat isn't likely to stay still long enough for you to do a thorough job.

- Start with gentle strokes, using a brush designed for your cat's coat type. Short-haired cats usually fare well with a rubber or bristle brush, while long-haired cats may require a slicker brush to manage their denser fur.

- Speak softly and reassuringly. Your voice has a remarkable ability to soothe your pet, making the grooming process more enjoyable.

- Reward your cat with treats and praise throughout the session, ensuring that they associate grooming time with positive experiences.

Trimming nails and cleaning ears are essential aspects of grooming that contribute to your cat's overall hygiene. Long nails can cause injuries or even grow into their paw pads, leading to painful infections. Similarly, clean ears are crucial to preventing mites, wax buildup, and potential infections.

To trim those claws without drama:

- Find a quiet spot and let your cat sit comfortably on your lap. You might want to swaddle them loosely in a towel if they tend to squirm.

- Gently press each toe pad until the nail extends, revealing the quick—the pink area you should avoid cutting.

- Trim just the tip of each claw, taking care not to nick the quick. If you do accidentally cut too far, use styptic powder or stick to stop any bleeding.

- Offer plenty of treats as you progress. Positive reinforcement goes a long way in making nail trims less daunting.

For ear cleaning:

- Examine your cat's ears weekly. Healthy ears should be pale pink and have no odor or debris.

- If there's noticeable dirt or wax, dab a cotton ball with a vet-recommended ear cleaner and wipe away the grime. Avoid using cotton swabs, as you risk damaging the ear canal.

- Monitor for signs of ear problems like persistent scratching, head shaking, or discharge, and consult your vet if anything seems off.

Recognizing signs of discomfort during grooming can help tailor the experience to your cat's preferences. Each cat has its own quirks and sensitivities, and recognizing these can make grooming more effective and less stressful for both parties.

Consider the following tips:

- Pay attention to body language. If your cat tenses up, flicks its tail rapidly, or tries to escape, take a break and resume later.

- Experiment with different brushes or techniques. Some cats prefer softer brushes, while others might enjoy a firmer touch.

- Keep sessions short initially. Gradually increase the length as your cat becomes more accustomed to the process.

- Never force a grooming session. If your cat shows signs of distress, stop and try again later. Their comfort and safety always come first.

Proper grooming practices can enhance your cat's well-being and strengthen the bond between you and your pet. Just as we humans feel better after a refreshing shower and a good haircut, cats thrive with regular grooming. Beyond physical benefits, the emotional connection fostered during these sessions can deepen your relationship with your furry friend.

Incorporating grooming into your routine might seem daunting at first, especially if you're dealing with a particularly feisty feline. However, patience and persistence will pay off. By making grooming a positive, regular activity, you ensure your cat remains healthy, happy, and looking their absolute best.

Remember, grooming isn't just an obligation —it's an opportunity for quality one-on-one time with your cat. These moments, filled with gentle brushes and soft murmurs, can become cherished rituals that both you and your pet look forward to. So grab that comb, settle into a cozy nook, and watch as your bond with your feline friend grows stronger with each stroke.

It's worth noting that the importance of grooming extends beyond individual cases. According to the ASPCA, many pet owners lack access to necessary grooming services and supplies, which can lead to neglect and health issues for pets (ASPCA Professional, 2022). Increasing awareness and resources related to grooming is paramount in supporting the well-being of our beloved companions.

If your cat ever shows signs of over-grooming themselves or neglect in their grooming habits, consider visiting a veterinarian. Changes in grooming behavior can often indicate underlying health issues, such as stress or pain (Does Your Cat Have a Grooming Problem?, n.d.). Being proactive in addressing these changes ensures that your cat maintains optimal health and happiness.

So, armed with a brush, some treats, and a heart full of love, step into the world of feline grooming with confidence. Your cat—and your bond with them—will undoubtedly flourish.

Appropriate Dietary Considerations and Weight Management

Feeding your cat isn't just about keeping their bowl full; it's a science. It starts with recognizing that cats are obligate carnivores. This means that unlike us or even our canine friends, cats thrive on a diet rich in animal proteins and fats. They genuinely don't do as well on high-carb meals. Think of them as little lions prowling through your living room—they need meat to stay at their healthiest.

Understanding this is the foundation for providing a balanced, species-appropriate diet. Commercial cat food often comes labeled with buzzwords like "complete" or "balanced," but not all kibble is created equal. Wet foods generally offer more protein and fewer carbs, aligning better with what cats would naturally eat in the wild.

Now, onto the heavier—pun intended—subject of weight management. Cat obesity isn't just an aesthetic issue; it's a serious health concern. Carrying extra pounds can predispose your cat to conditions like diabetes, arthritis, and even certain cancers (Association for Pet Obesity Prevention, n.d.). The stakes are high, but the good news is you have the power to keep your furry friend in top shape.

Here's a simple guideline to monitor and manage your cat's weight:

- Start by weighing your cat regularly. Make it part of your monthly routine to jump on the scale together.

- Adjust feeding portions based on your cat's activity level and weight goals. It's not about starving them but finding a balance.

- Use a proper measuring cup to avoid overfeeding. You'd be surprised how easy it is to give an extra scoop when eyeballing it.

- If you're unsure, consult your vet to calculate daily caloric needs. Trust me, they'll break it down like a feline nutritionist!

Speaking of vet consultations, these professionals are indispensable in tailoring diets for specific needs. Whether you have a rambunctious kitten or an elderly cat dealing with kidney issues, a one-size-fits-all approach doesn't cut it. Your veterinarian can recommend specialized diets that address unique requirements, ensuring each stage of your cat's life is met with the right nutrition.

For specialized dietary needs:

- Schedule regular vet visits to discuss changing dietary requirements.
- Get blood work done periodically to identify deficiencies or health conditions early.
- Ask for recommendations on therapeutic diets if your cat has health issues.

Beyond just the food, how you feed your cat also matters. Interactive feeding methods can transform meal times from mundane to enriching experiences. Cats are natural hunters, and engaging their predatory instincts makes eating much more stimulating.

To incorporate interactive feeding methods:

- Use puzzle feeders that slow down eating and make mealtime a mental exercise.
- Rotate the location of food bowls to encourage movement. A little dash upstairs or downstairs could be the mini workout they need.
- Try DIY options like hiding food around the house. It turns dinner into a treasure hunt!
- Start using treat balls that dispense kibbles only when batted around.

Add a dash of playtime, and you've got a recipe for a happy, healthy cat. Exercise is key. Aim for 15-20 minutes of play every day, divided into short, exciting bursts. Feather toys, laser pointers, or anything that mimics prey can turn your lazy indoor kitty into an agile hunter again.

Also, let's not forget about hydration. Cats often don't drink enough water, especially if they're on a dry food diet. Adding water fountains can make drinking more appealing. They love the running water—it attracts them naturally. Plus, wet foods help boost their fluid intake. Aim for a mix to ensure they're well-hydrated.

Feeding multiple cats? I've been there— juggling meals can get chaotic. The simplest solution is feeding each cat separately. Not only does this prevent the chubbier ones from snagging extra bites, but it ensures everyone gets their fair share. And if you have an overweight cat, put their bowl in a less accessible spot. These small changes can make a world of difference.

Cats begging for food are another challenge. They're excellent manipulators—those big eyes staring up at you, pleading for just one more treat. It's tough, I know. But giving in can sabotage even the best-laid plans. Instead, swap food begging with affection. Play with them, pet them, or just spend time cuddling. Many cats crave attention more than food (though they'd never admit it).

Remember, cats aren't small dogs. What works for Fido won't necessarily work for Fluffy. Understanding their unique nutritional needs, monitoring their weight, and adjusting their diets are crucial steps towards a long, healthy life. A little effort on your part can ward off numerous health issues, ensuring many joyful years together.

In the end, proper nutrition and weight management are the cornerstones of your cat's health and longevity. Every kibble you measure, every pound you track, and every vet visit you make contributes to their well-being. It's a journey, but one that rewards both of you immensely. So, gear up, grab that measuring cup, and let's keep our furry friends purring and playful for years to come!

Recognizing Behavioral Indicators of Health Concerns

Changes in your cat's behavior can often serve as subtle signals of underlying health issues. If you start noticing that your kitty's eating habits have changed or your kitty isn't pouncing on his favorite toy mouse with the same enthusiasm, it's worth paying attention.

Take eating, for example. Cats are creatures of habit, and any deviation from their regular eating patterns might be a red flag. Increased or decreased appetite can signify anything from dental problems to gastrointestinal issues (Countryside Veterinary Clinic, 2023). Similarly, if you notice your feline friend is drinking more or less than usual, this could indicate conditions like diabetes or kidney disease. And let's not forget the litter box—changes in litter box habits, such as urinating outside the box or straining to go, can be indicative of urinary tract problems.

But it's not just about food and bathroom behaviors. Social interactions can also give you clues. If your cat suddenly becomes a recluse, hiding under the bed all day, or turns into a social butterfly who won't leave your side, these shifts may hint at anxiety or stress-related health issues.

The key here is to know what is normal for your cat so you can spot when something's off.

Monitoring your cat's behavior requires keen observation skills. You don't need to become Sherlock Holmes, but being a bit more attentive can make a world of difference. Cats are masters at hiding discomfort; they've got an Oscar-deserving ability to mask pain. According to Best Friends Veterinary Hospital, changes in grooming habits can reveal a lot about your cat's well-being. If they suddenly stop grooming themselves, appearing more like a disheveled ball of fur rather than their usual sleek selves, they could be in pain or distress. Conversely, over-grooming one area could indicate skin issues or allergies (KimS, 2024).

Listen closely to your cat's vocalizations too. A usually quiet cat who starts meowing excessively or making strange noises might be trying to tell you something's wrong. Physical signs like limping, difficulty jumping, or even subtle changes in breathing patterns can also be signals worth noting.

Now, if you do notice behavioral changes in your furry companion, it's crucial to consult with a veterinarian promptly. Early diagnosis and treatment can significantly impact your cat's health. Here's how to approach this:

- First, observe and note any specific changes in behavior. Was it sudden or gradual? How long has it been going on?

- Second, communicate these changes clearly to your vet. Providing detailed observations can help them diagnose the issue more accurately.

- Third, follow up on any tests or treatments recommended by your veterinarian to ensure your cat is on the path to recovery.

In addition to timely veterinary consultations, keeping a health journal for your cat can be incredibly beneficial. This doesn't mean turning your home into a full-scale laboratory, but a simple notebook where you jot down any deviations from your cat's usual routines can be a valuable tool. Imagine your vet's relief when you walk in with a record saying, "Yes, Doctor, Snowball's been eating less since Tuesday, sleeping more in the afternoons, and has shown unusual reluctance to jump onto her favorite perch."

Here's what you can do to maintain a helpful health journal:

- Record daily observations of your cat's eating, drinking, and litter box habits or deviation from the usual.

- Note any unusual vocalizations or physical signs of discomfort.

- Include remarks on social interactions and changes in activity levels.

- Update the journal during veterinary visits with diagnoses, treatments, and follow-up care instructions.

Keeping a health journal isn't about being meticulous just for the sake of it. It's about providing a comprehensive picture to your vet, which can make diagnosing and treating any issues far more effective.

Understanding your cat's normal behavior is the first step toward recognizing when something might be wrong. By staying observant and proactive, you can play a significant role in maintaining your cat's health and well-being. After all, our feline friends rely on us to interpret their subtle cues and ensure they lead happy, healthy lives.

Concluding Thoughts on Cat Health and Well-Being

Maintaining your cat's health and well-being might sound like a daunting task, but armed with the right knowledge, it's more like plotting to knock a potted plant off the shelf—satisfyingly challenging yet entirely doable. Throughout this chapter, we've navigated the essential guidelines for keeping your feline friend happy and healthy.

We began by emphasizing the importance of regular veterinary care. Cats are experts at hiding discomfort, so those seemingly dreadful vet visits can catch lurking health issues before they become full-blown catastrophes. Think of these check-ups as preventive strikes against potential sneaky ailments. From heart murmurs to dental woes, early detection is key.

We also dived into preventive treatments to keep the creepy crawlies at bay. Fleas, ticks, and heartworms can turn your cat's life—and yours—upside down quicker than you can open a can of tuna. Vaccinations play a superstar role too, donning your feline in a superhero cape that shields against dangerous diseases. By establishing a trusting relationship with your vet, you transform these visits from stress-inducing episodes to smooth sailing routines.

Understanding your cat's age and breed-specific needs was another crucial point we covered. Whether dealing with a playful kitten or an elegant senior cat, tailoring care to their unique requirements ensures they thrive at each life stage. And speaking of thriving, recognizing any changes in your cat's behavior can be a game-changer. Whether it's tweaking diet portions or spotting unusual grooming habits, a little observation goes a long way.

Now, as you cuddle up with your content kitty purring softly beside you, remember that maintaining their health isn't just about avoiding problems—it's about enhancing the quality of their nine lives (and your one). Proactive care keeps your bond strong and ensures more sunny afternoons watching the world together from a cozy windowsill.

So, dear cat parent, heed these guidelines with humor and heart. Your efforts will result in a happier, healthier companion who continues to bring joy, mischief, and love into your life. Because, at the end of the day, every purr, every head-bump, and every playful flick of the tail counts. Keep those tails high, those whiskers twitching, and stay weird!

Breed Specific Behavior

We hope you've gained understanding of your cat's quirky behavior. This does help embrace the weird and find acceptance. If only the human world could function with as much understanding, wouldn't that enrich our health and well-being too? Picture this: an environment where humans are valued as individuals, each one with quirks and differences everyone observes and appreciates. We could learn so much from our feline friends. But I digress. Providing a space where your cat feels most comfortable will not only contribute to their health and well-being but rewards you with love and warmth in a place you will enjoy as home, sweet home. As pet owners, it's important to understand the distinct characteristics of different cat breeds to provide the best possible care and companionship.

From the regal Maine Coon to the playful Siamese, the cat kingdom boasts a diverse array of breeds, each with their own endearing behavior patterns. The Persian, known for its luxurious coat and gentle demeanor, may require more grooming attention than the independent-minded British Shorthair. Meanwhile, the Abyssinian's curious nature and love of heights can keep owners on their toes.

Recognizing these breed-specific tendencies is key to fostering a harmonious and fulfilling relationship with your feline friend. Whether you're an experienced cat parent or a first-time owner, familiarizing yourself with the common behavior quirks of various cat breeds can help you anticipate your pet's needs and create a truly rewarding partnership.

Here are some common cat breeds and their quirky behaviors:

· Siamese: Siamese cats are known for being vocal and social. They often "talk" to their owners with loud meows and are quite demanding for attention, akin to the cat we endearingly called "Punt."

· Maine Coon: Maine Coons are large, friendly cats known for their playful nature. They are also skilled hunters and may bring their owners "presents" such as toys or even small prey.

· Scottish Fold: Scottish Folds are recognized by their unique folded ears. They are known for their love of sitting in unusual positions, such as perching on their hind legs or sleeping with their paws covering their faces.

· Sphynx: Sphynx cats are hairless and have a warm body temperature. They are often found seeking out cozy spots in the house, such as sunbeams or under blankets. They are subject of much garment wearing to aid in holding in their warmth, if not fulfilling the fashion whimsy of their owners.

· Bengal: Bengals are energetic and intelligent cats with a love for water. They may enjoy playing in sinks or even joining their owners in the shower

· Persian: Persians are known for their long, luxurious coats and sweet personalities. They are often found lounging in regal poses and may be picky about grooming.

· Russian Blue: Russian Blues are intelligent and independent cats. They are known for their love of play and may even learn to fetch toys like a dog.

· Ragdoll: Ragdolls are gentle and affectionate cats that often go limp when picked up, hence their name. They enjoy being held and may follow their owners around the house like a loyal companion.

· American Shorthair: American Shorthairs are versatile and adaptable cats. They are known for their hunting instincts and may enjoy chasing toys or even insects around the house.

· Tabby: Tabby cats come in various colors and patterns, but they are often characterized by their "M" shaped markings on their foreheads. They are known for their playful and curious nature, often getting into mischief around the house.

· Abyssinian: Abyssinians are active and playful cats known for their love of climbing and exploring high places. They are curious and may even try to "help" their owners with tasks around the house.

· Burmese: Burmese cats are affectionate and social. They are often described as "dog-like" for their loyalty and tendency to follow their owners from room to room. They may even enjoy playing fetch with their favorite toys.

· British Shorthair: British Shorthairs are calm and easygoing cats. They are known for their round faces and chunky bodies. They may have a laid-back attitude but can also be quite playful, especially when it comes to interactive toys.

· Siberian: Siberian cats are known for their thick, water-resistant fur and playful personalities. They are agile climbers and may enjoy perching on high vantage points to observe their surroundings.

· Norwegian Forest Cat: Norwegian Forest Cats are large, fluffy cats with a love for the outdoors. They are skilled hunters and may bring their owners "gifts" from their adventures outside.

Conclusion

The feline world is akin to a box of chocolates, you never know what you're going to get! Even the number of cat breeds can vary depending on which cat association you ask, but as of 2023, the International Cat Association (TICA) recognizes 73 standardized breeds, while the Cat Fanciers' Association (CFA) recognizes 45. Other well-recognized registries and associations fall between these numbers, such as the Fédération Internationale Féline, which recognizes 48 breeds. The exact number of breeds can fluctuate slightly depending on the cat association and their criteria. Besides, let's not forget about those quirky personalities that make each tiny soul an individual.

In conclusion, I hope you can now understand the reason for some weird cat behavior and learned practical tips and tricks that are affordable and easy to implement in your life and environment that will strengthen your bond and enrich your lives, health, and well-being.

We only get to spend a portion of our lives with our feline friends. Let's make each day count.

One last thought: just when you think you've got your kitty figured out, they change things up on you.

Such is the nature of a cat, keeping it *weird* .

Bibliography

Raw *Meat-Based Diets for Pets* . WSAVA Global Nutrition Committee., Apr. 2021, WSAVAhttps://wsava.org/wp-content/uploads/2021/04/Raw-Meat-Based-Diets-for-Pets_WSAVA-Global-Nutrition-Toolkit.pdf.

"10 Cat & Dog Holiday Treat Recipes." *The Animal Foundation* , https://animalfoundation.com/whats-going-on/blog/10-cat-dog-treat-recipes-holidays. Accessed 25 May 2024.

Alegría-Morán, Raúl A., et al. "Food Preferences in Cats: Effect of Dietary Composition and Intrinsic Variables on Diet Selection." *Animals* , vol. 9, no. 6, June 2019, p. 372. *DOI.org (Crossref)* , https://doi.org/10.3390/ani9060372.

Animals, Michelson Found. "Easy Holiday Dog (and Cat) Treat Recipes." *Michelson Found Animals* , 14 Nov. 2019, https://www.foundanimals.org/easy-holiday-dog-and-cat-treat-recipes/.

---. "How to Satisfy Your Cat's Natural Instincts." *Michelson Found Animals* , 23 May

2019, https://www.foundanimals.org/how-to-satisfy-your-cats-natural-instincts/.

anitadib. "The Ultimate Guide To Cat Shelves on Walls." *The Worth of Words - A Universal Blog of Life* , 24 May 2023, https://theworthofwords.org/the-ultimate-guide-to-cat-shelves-on-walls/.

Author, Guest. "Decoding Cat Body Language." *Cat Care Society* , 23 Aug. 2023, https://catcaresociety.org/decoding-cat-body-language/.

"Bengal Cat Blog Articles on Every Topic Related to Cats: Life Is Better With Bengals." *JEWELSPRIDE BENGALS* ,
https://www.jewelspridebengals.org/bengalcatarticles.html.
Accessed 25 May 2024.

Bjornvad, Charlotte, and Kirsten Madsen Hoelmkjaer. "Management of Obesity in Cats." *Veterinary Medicine: Research and Reports* , Sept. 2014, p. 97. *DOI.org (Crossref)* , https://doi.org/10.2147/VMRR.S40869.

Black Cat Dream Meaning - Religion and Gender . 14 May 2024, https://religionandgender.org/black-cat-dream-meaning/.

Bring Home the Catwalk: Stylish and Enriching Designs for the Feline-Friendly Home .
https://journal.iaabcfoundation.org/stylish-cat-enrichment/.
Accessed 25 May 2024.

Cat Communication | International Cat Care
.

https://icatcare.org/advice/cat-communication/.
Accessed 25 May 2024.

"Cat Confinement in a New Home." *San Diego Humane Society* , 7 Jan. 2022, https://resources.sdhumane.org/Resource_Center/Behavior_and_Training/Cats_and_Kittens/Adopting_a_Cat_Things_to_Consider/Cat_Confinement_in_a_New_Home.
Cat Grooming Tips | ASPCA .
https://www.aspca.org/pet-care/cat-care/cat-grooming-tips.
Accessed 25 May 2024.

"Cat Weight Loss Information." *Association for Pet Obesity Prevention* ,
https://www.petobesityprevention.org/weight-loss-cats.
Accessed 25 May 2024.

"Cats and Their Hunting Behaviour." *FOUR PAWS International - Animal Welfare Organisation* ,
https://www.four-paws.org/our-stories/publications-guides/cats-and-their-hunting-behaviour.
Accessed 25 May 2024.

"Common Cat Hazards." *Cornell University College of Veterinary Medicine* , 11 Oct. 2017, https://www.vet.cornell.edu/departments-centers-and-institutes/cornell-feline-health-center/health-information/feline-health-topics/common-cat-hazards.
Crazy for Catnip | The Humane Society of the United States .

https://www.humanesociety.org/resources/ crazy-catnip. Accessed 25 May 2024.

DACVIM (Nutrition), Deborah E. Linder, DVM, MS. "How Do I Get My Picky Pet to Eat?" *Clinical Nutrition Service at Cummings School* , 16 Mar. 2017, https://vetnutrition.tufts.edu/ 2017/03/how-do-i-get-my-picky-pet-to-eat/.
"Demystifying Feline Behavior." *Penn Today* , 19 Feb. 2020, https://penntoday.upenn.edu/ news/demystifying-feline-behavior.
"Do Animals Dream?" *Animals Now* , 23 Oct. 2023, https://animals-now.org/en/do-animals-dream/.
Does Your Cat Have a Grooming Problem? https://uptownvethospital.org/articles/ 530555-does-your-cat-have-a-grooming-problem. Accessed 25 May 2024.

"Dreaming of Cats - What Do Cat Dreams Mean?" *Mindberg* , 29 Jan. 2024, https:// mindberg.org/insights/dreaming-of-cats-what-do-cat-dreams-mean/.
"---." *Mindberg* , 29 Jan. 2024, https:// mindberg.org/insights/dreaming-of-cats-what-do-cat-dreams-mean/.
"Feeding Your Cat." *Cornell University College of Veterinary Medicine* , 16 Oct. 2017, https://www.vet.cornell.edu/departments-centers-and-institutes/cornell-feline-health-center/health-information/feline-health-topics/ feeding-your-cat.
"Feline Behavior Problems: Aggression." *Cornell University College of Veterinary Medicine* , 9 Oct. 2017, https://

www.vet.cornell.edu/departments-centers-and-institutes/cornell-feline-health-center/health-information/feline-health-topics/feline-behavior-problems-aggression.

Fermo, Jaciana Luzia, et al. "Only When It Feels Good: Specific Cat Vocalizations Other Than Meowing." *Animals* , vol. 9, no. 11, Oct. 2019, p. 878. *DOI.org (Crossref)* , https://doi.org/10.3390/ani9110878.

Filipino Doctors . n.d., https://medicalbooks.filipinodoctors.org/item/1601383983.

Five Scientific Studies Unraveling Dream Symbols - Religion and Gender . 20 Jan. 2024, https://religionandgender.org/five-scientific-studies-unraveling-dream-symbols/.

Foundation, The Animal Health. "Study: Cats May Not Be as Aloof as They Seem." *The Animal Health Foundation* , 28 June 2013, https://www.animalhealthfoundation.org/blog/2013/06/study-cats-may-not-be-as-aloof-as-they-seem/.

Gajdoš Kmecová, Noema, et al. "Are These Cats Playing? A Closer Look at Social Play in Cats and Proposal for a Psychobiological Approach and Standard Terminology." *Frontiers in Veterinary Science* , vol. 8, July 2021, p. 712310. *DOI.org (Crossref)* , https://doi.org/10.3389/fvets.2021.712310.

González-Ramírez, Mónica Teresa, and René Landero-Hernández. "Cat Coat Color, Personality Traits and the Cat-Owner Relationship Scale: A Study with Cat Owners in Mexico." *Animals* , vol. 12, no. 8, Apr. 2022, p. 1030. *DOI.org (Crossref)* , https://doi.org/10.3390/ani12081030.

Help Your Cat Use the Litter Box | Humane Society of the United States .

https://www.humanesociety.org/resources/
how-help-your-cats-use-litter-box.
Accessed 25 May 2024.

Household Hazards | American Veterinary Medical Association .
https://www.avma.org/resources-tools/pet-owners/petcare/household-hazards.
Accessed 25 May 2024.

How to Read Your Cat's Body Language | Animal Humane Society .
https://www.animalhumanesociety.org/resource/how-read-your-cats-body-language.
Accessed 25 May 2024.

Humane Handling of Cats: How To Do 4 Safe & Effective Holds | ASPCApro . 10 Apr. 2017, https://www.aspcapro.org/catholds.
Humphrey, Tasmin, et al. "The Role of Cat Eye Narrowing Movements in Cat–Human Communication." *Scientific Reports* , vol. 10, no. 1, Oct. 2020, p. 16503. *DOI.org (Crossref)* , https://doi.org/10.1038/s41598-020-73426-0.
Hunting Enrichment for Indoor Cats Part 1: Indoor Activities .
https://journal.iaabcfoundation.org/hunting-enrichment-for-indoor-cats-part-1/.
Accessed 25 May 2024.

Inc, Our Healthy Communities. "5 SIMPLE LITTER BOX TIPS." *OHCNWA* , 11 Oct. 2021, https://www.ohcnwa.org/post/5-simple-litter-box-tips.
Increase Access to Dog and Cat Grooming Services to Improve Animal Health | ASPCApro . 28 Feb. 2022, https://www.aspcapro.org/

resource/increase-access-dog-and-cat-grooming-services-improve-animal-health.

Ines, Mauro, et al. "My Cat and Me—A Study of Cat Owner Perceptions of Their Bond and Relationship." *Animals* , vol. 11, no. 6, May 2021, p. 1601. *DOI.org (Crossref)* , https://doi.org/ 10.3390/ani11061601.

"Is Your Cat Acting Strange? Behavior Changes That Are a Red Flag." *Countryside Veterinary Clinic* , 7 July 2023, https:// www.countrysideveterinaryclinic.org/services/ cats/blog/your-cat-acting-strange-behavior-changes-are-red-flag.

KimS. "Detecting Subtle Indicators of Pain or Discomfort in Cats." *Best Friends Veterinary Hospital* , 15 Feb. 2024, https:// bestfriendsvet.org/blog/how-to-tell-if-a-cat-is-in-pain/.

Knight, Andrew, and Madelaine Leitsberger. "Vegetarian versus Meat-Based Diets for Companion Animals." *Animals* , vol. 6, no. 9, Sept. 2016, p. 57. *DOI.org (Crossref)* , https:// doi.org/10.3390/ani6090057.

Less Affectionate Cat - Cat Chat Feline Forum . https://www.catchat.org/felineforum/ viewtopic.php?t=11014. Accessed 25 May 2024.

Litchfield, Carla A., et al. "The 'Feline Five': An Exploration of Personality in Pet Cats (Felis Catus)." *PLOS ONE* , edited by Christopher A. Lepczyk, vol. 12, no. 8, Aug. 2017, p. e0183455. *DOI.org (Crossref)* , https://doi.org/10.1371/ journal.pone.0183455.

"Litter Box Tips." *Maddie's Fund* ,

https://www.maddiesfund.org/kb-litter-box-tips.htm.
Accessed 25 May 2024.

Martínez-Byer, Sandra, et al. "Evidence for Individual Differences in Behaviour and for Behavioural Syndromes in Adult Shelter Cats." *Animals* , vol. 10, no. 6, June 2020, p. 962. *DOI.org (Crossref)* , https://doi.org/10.3390/ani10060962.
Mikkola, Salla, et al. "Reliability and Validity of Seven Feline Behavior and Personality Traits." *Animals* , vol. 11, no. 7, July 2021, p. 1991. *DOI.org (Crossref)* , https://doi.org/10.3390/ani11071991.
Noreika, Valdas, et al. "Modulating Dream Experience: Noninvasive Brain Stimulation over the Sensorimotor Cortex Reduces Dream Movement." *Scientific Reports* , vol. 10, no. 1, Apr. 2020, p. 6735. *DOI.org (Crossref)* , https://doi.org/10.1038/s41598-020-63479-6.
orzechowski, karol. "Our Intertwined Evolution With Cats." *Faunalytics* , 16 Dec. 2015, https://faunalytics.org/intertwined-evolution-cats/.
Outfitting and Enriching Communal Cat Rooms | ASPCApro . 17 Apr. 2015, https://www.aspcapro.org/outfitting-and-enriching-communal-cat-rooms.
--- . 17 Apr. 2015, https://www.aspcapro.org/outfitting-and-enriching-communal-cat-rooms.
Pack, Carrie. "Want Healthy, Happy Cats? Let Them Play with Their Food." *Adventure Cats* , 10 Feb. 2019, https://www.adventurecats.org/indoor-adventures/want-healthy-happy-cats-let-them-play-with-their-food/.

Prato-Previde, Emanuela, et al. "What's in a Meow? A Study on Human Classification and Interpretation of Domestic Cat Vocalizations." *Animals* , vol. 10, no. 12, Dec. 2020, p. 2390. *DOI.org (Crossref)* , https://doi.org/10.3390/ani10122390.

Rescue, SAFe. "Household Hazards for Cats • Seattle Area Feline Rescue." *Seattle Area Feline Rescue* , 17 Mar. 2023, https://www.seattleareafelinerescue.org/household-hazards-for-cats/.

Ruby, Perrine M. "Experimental Research on Dreaming: State of the Art and Neuropsychoanalytic Perspectives." *Frontiers in Psychology* , vol. 2, 2011. *DOI.org (Crossref)* , https://doi.org/10.3389/fpsyg.2011.00286.

Seeing Cat in Dream Spiritual Meaning - Religion and Gender . 19 Apr. 2024, https://religionandgender.org/seeing-cat-in-dream-spiritual-meaning/.

SITNFlash. "The Cat's out of the Bag! Why Cats Can't Get Enough of Catnip." *Science in the News* , 4 Jan. 2024, https://sitn.hms.harvard.edu/flash/2024/the-cats-out-of-the-bag-the-biological-reason-why-cats-cant-get-enough-of-catnip/.

Ståhl, Aada, et al. "Pet and Owner Personality and Mental Wellbeing Associate with Attachment to Cats and Dogs." *iScience* , vol. 26, no. 12, Dec. 2023, p. 108423. *DOI.org (Crossref)* , https://doi.org/10.1016/j.isci.2023.108423.

Stogdale, Lea. "One Veterinarian's Experience with Owners Who Are Feeding Raw Meat to Their Pets." *The Canadian Veterinary Journal* , vol. 60, no. 6, June 2019, pp. 655–58.

PubMed Central , https://www.ncbi.nlm.nih.gov/pmc/articles/PMC6515799/.

Syndram, Lourdes. "The Purr-Fect Practice: Why Regular Vet Visits Are Essential for Your Feline Friend." *INVMA* , 26 July 2023, https://invma.org/the-purr-fect-practice-why-regular-vet-visits-are-essential-for-your-feline-friend/.

Tavernier, Chloé, et al. "Feline Vocal Communication." *Journal of Veterinary Science* , vol. 21, no. 1, 2020, p. e18. *DOI.org (Crossref)* , https://doi.org/10.4142/jvs.2020.21.e18.

Texas A&M University College of Veterinary Medicine & Biomedical Sciences. "Feline Fine: The Benefits of Catnip." *VMBS News* , 5 Dec. 2019, https://vetmed.tamu.edu/news/pet-talk/feline-fine-the-benefits-of-catnip/.

"The Cat Socialization Continuum: A Guide to Interactions Between Cats and Humans." *Alley Cat Allies* ,
https://www.alleycat.org/resources/cat-socialization-continuum-guide/.
Accessed 25 May 2024.

"The History of the Domestic Cat." *Alley Cat Allies* ,
https://www.alleycat.org/resources/the-natural-history-of-the-cat/.
Accessed 25 May 2024.

"The Joys of Owning a Cat - HelpGuide.Org." *Https://Www.Helpguide.Org* ,
https://www.helpguide.org/articles/healthy-living/joys-of-owning-a-cat.htm.
Accessed 25 May 2024.

They Did It: Creating More Vertical Space for Cats | ASPCApro . 1 May 2017, https://

www.aspcapro.org/resource/they-did-it-creating-more-vertical-space-cats.

Translating Feline Body Language | PAWS Chicago .
https://www.pawschicago.org/news-resources/all-about-cats/understanding-cat-behavior/translating-feline-body-language/showpage.
Accessed 25 May 2024.

Understanding Feline Language | The Humane Society of the United States .
https://www.humanesociety.org/resources/understanding-feline-language.
Accessed 25 May 2024.

--- .
https://www.humanesociety.org/resources/understanding-feline-language.
Accessed 25 May 2024.

Vitale, Kristyn R., et al. "Attachment Bonds between Domestic Cats and Humans." *Current Biology* , vol. 29, no. 18, Sept. 2019, pp. R864–65. *DOI.org (Crossref)* , https://doi.org/10.1016/j.cub.2019.08.036.
---. "Attachment Bonds between Domestic Cats and Humans." *Current Biology* , vol. 29, no. 18, Sept. 2019, pp. R864–65. *DOI.org (Crossref)* , https://doi.org/10.1016/j.cub.2019.08.036.
"Why Are Regular Veterinary Visits Important?" *AAHA* , 9 Apr. 2020, https://www.aaha.org/resources/why-are-regular-veterinary-visits-important/.
Why Routine Preventative Care for Your Pet Is Essential | Animal Humane Society .

https://www.animalhumanesociety.org/
resource/why-routine-preventative-care-your-
pet-essential.
Accessed 25 May 2024.

"WSAVA Global Nutrition Committee.
(2021). Raw Meat-Based Diets for Pets. ." *WSAVA
Global Nutrition Committee. (2021). Raw Meat-
Based Diets for Pets. Retrieved from Https://
wsaRaw-Meat-Based-Diets-for-Pets_WSAVA-
Global-Nutrition-Toolkit.Pdf* , 2021.

Wu, Katherine J. "Cats Give the Laws of
Physics a Biiiiig Stretch." *The Atlantic* , 13 Sept.
2022, https://www.theatlantic.com/science/
archive/2022/09/falling-dropped-cat-reflex-
physics/671424/.

About the Author

L. R. Susko, born in Pittsburgh, Pennsylvania, is a seasoned pharmacist and Duquesne University graduate with over 30 years of experience. Licensed to practice in multiple states, L.R. Susko is a lifelong animal lover and a cancer survivor of 5 years. A parent to one adult son and 4 weird cats, L.R. Susko is known for their never-ending curiosity and conversation. Their writing style is educational, entertaining, and humorous. Although new to self-publishing, L.R. Susko's talent was evident from a young age, with their first submission appearing in Apple Magazine at just 12 years of age.